OPTIONS TRADING JOURNAL

USE THIS TRADING JOURNAL FOR EVERY TRADE TO ACHIEVE TRADING SUCCESS.
(200 TRADES)

LR THOMAS

DEDICATION

THIS BOOK IS DEDICATED TO ALL OPTIONS TRADERS WHO WANT TO ACHIEVE EXCELLENCE.

I WISH YOU ALL THE BEST ON YOUR TRADING JOURNEY.

LR THOMAS

ALL RIGHTS RESERVED. NO PART OF THIS PUBLICATION MAY BE REPRODUCED IN ANY FORM OR BY ANY MEANS, INCLUDING SCANNING, PHOTOCOPYING, OR OTHERWISE WITHOUT PRIOR WRITTEN PERMISSION OF THE COPYRIGHT HOLDER. COPYRIGHT © 2017 LR THOMAS

HOW TO USE THIS JOURNAL

RECORD EVERY TRADE GOOD OR BAD SO YOU CAN LOOK FOR PATTERNS THAT YOU CAN IMPROVE ON

WHEN YOU ARE RECORDING YOUR TRADES, ADD THE EMOTIONS YOU WERE FEELING AND THE THOUGHTS THAT CAME UP SO YOU CAN SEE THEM IN THE COLD LIGHT OF DAY WHEN YOU GO BACK OVER YOUR TRADES.

MAKE IT YOUR GOAL TO LEARN FROM EVERY TRADE AND USE THAT KNOWLEDGE TO IMPROVE YOUR NEXT TRADE.

DATE _____ TIME _____

DEMO/REAL   INSTRUMENT _____

SETUP
_____
_____
_____

A/B/C GRADE TRADE   RANDOM TRADE?
STOP ADHERED TO Y/N
IF NOT WHY NOT?
_____
_____
_____

TAKE PROFIT ADHERED TO Y/N
IF NOT WHY NOT?
_____
_____
_____

BREAK EVEN ADHERED TO Y/N
IF NOT WHY NOT?
_____
_____
_____

LESSONS I LEARNED FROM THIS TRADE
_____
_____
_____
_____
_____
_____

WIN/LOSS _____
PROFIT % ON ACCOUNT _____
LOSS % ON ACCOUNT _____

HOW WILL I IMPROVE ON MY NEXT TRADE
_____
_____
_____

VISUAL EXCERCISE (5-10 MINUTES)

PUT ON SOME SOFT MUSIC, LAY BACK AND RELAX AND RECREATE THE TRADE IN YOUR MIND'S EYE.

NOW SEE YOURSELF GOING THROUGH A TRADE BUT NOW YOU ARE IMPLEMENTING THE NEW LESSONS LEARNED FROM THIS TRADE. REPEAT UNTIL YOU AUTOMATICALLY ACT THIS WAY DURING TRADES

TRADER AFFIRMATIONS (SAY 100 TIMES A DAY)

I AM A GREAT TRADER/ I LEARN LESSONS FROM EVERY TRADE AND IMPLEMENT THEM/ I AM A CONSTANTLY IMPROVING TRADER/ I AIM FOR EXCELLENCE IN EVERY TRADE.

DATE _____ TIME _____

DEMO/REAL   INSTRUMENT _____

SETUP
_____
_____
_____

A/B/C GRADE TRADE   RANDOM TRADE?

STOP ADHERED TO Y/N

IF NOT WHY NOT?
_____
_____
_____

TAKE PROFIT ADHERED TO Y/N

IF NOT WHY NOT?
_____
_____
_____

BREAK EVEN ADHERED TO Y/N

IF NOT WHY NOT?
_____
_____
_____

LESSONS I LEARNED FROM THIS TRADE

_____
_____
_____
_____
_____
_____

WIN/LOSS _____
PROFIT % ON ACCOUNT _____
LOSS % ON ACCOUNT _____

HOW WILL I IMPROVE ON MY NEXT TRADE
_____
_____
_____

VISUAL EXCERCISE (5-10 MINUTES)

PUT ON SOME SOFT MUSIC, LAY BACK AND RELAX AND RECREATE THE TRADE IN YOUR MIND'S EYE.
NOW SEE YOURSELF GOING THROUGH A TRADE BUT NOW YOU ARE IMPLEMENTING THE NEW LESSONS LEARNED FROM THIS TRADE. REPEAT UNTIL YOU AUTOMATICALLY ACT THIS WAY DURING TRADES

TRADER AFFIRMATIONS (SAY 100 TIMES A DAY)

I AM A GREAT TRADER/ I LEARN LESSONS FROM EVERY TRADE AND IMPLEMENT THEM/ I AM A CONSTANTLY IMPROVING TRADER/ I AIM FOR EXCELLENCE IN EVERY TRADE.

DATE _____   TIME _____

DEMO/REAL   INSTRUMENT _____

SETUP
_____
_____
_____

A/B/C GRADE TRADE   RANDOM TRADE?
STOP ADHERED TO Y/N
IF NOT WHY NOT?
_____
_____
_____

TAKE PROFIT ADHERED TO Y/N
IF NOT WHY NOT?
_____
_____
_____

BREAK EVEN ADHERED TO Y/N
IF NOT WHY NOT?
_____
_____
_____

LESSONS I LEARNED FROM THIS TRADE

_____
_____
_____
_____
_____
_____

WIN/LOSS _____

PROFIT % ON ACCOUNT _____

LOSS % ON ACCOUNT _____

HOW WILL I IMPROVE ON MY NEXT TRADE

_____
_____
_____

VISUAL EXCERCISE (5-10 MINUTES)

PUT ON SOME SOFT MUSIC, LAY BACK AND RELAX AND RECREATE THE TRADE IN YOUR MIND'S EYE.

NOW SEE YOURSELF GOING THROUGH A TRADE BUT NOW YOU ARE IMPLEMENTING THE NEW LESSONS LEARNED FROM THIS TRADE. REPEAT UNTIL YOU AUTOMATICALLY ACT THIS WAY DURING TRADES

TRADER AFFIRMATIONS (SAY 100 TIMES A DAY)

I AM A GREAT TRADER/ I LEARN LESSONS FROM EVERY TRADE AND IMPLEMENT THEM/ I AM A CONSTANTLY IMPROVING TRADER/ I AIM FOR EXCELLENCE IN EVERY TRADE.

DATE _____   TIME _____

DEMO/REAL   INSTRUMENT _____

SETUP
_____
_____
_____

A/B/C GRADE TRADE   RANDOM TRADE?

STOP ADHERED TO Y/N

IF NOT WHY NOT?
_____
_____
_____

TAKE PROFIT ADHERED TO Y/N

IF NOT WHY NOT?
_____
_____
_____

BREAK EVEN ADHERED TO Y/N

IF NOT WHY NOT?
_____
_____
_____

LESSONS I LEARNED FROM THIS TRADE

_____
_____
_____
_____
_____
_____

WIN/LOSS _____
PROFIT % ON ACCOUNT _____
LOSS % ON ACCOUNT _____

HOW WILL I IMPROVE ON MY NEXT TRADE

_____
_____
_____

VISUAL EXCERCISE (5-10 MINUTES)

PUT ON SOME SOFT MUSIC, LAY BACK AND RELAX AND RECREATE THE TRADE IN YOUR MIND'S EYE.

NOW SEE YOURSELF GOING THROUGH A TRADE BUT NOW YOU ARE IMPLEMENTING THE NEW LESSONS LEARNED FROM THIS TRADE. REPEAT UNTIL YOU AUTOMATICALLY ACT THIS WAY DURING TRADES

TRADER AFFIRMATIONS (SAY 100 TIMES A DAY)

I AM A GREAT TRADER/ I LEARN LESSONS FROM EVERY TRADE AND IMPLEMENT THEM/ I AM A CONSTANTLY IMPROVING TRADER/ I AIM FOR EXCELLENCE IN EVERY TRADE.

DATE _____ TIME _____

DEMO/REAL   INSTRUMENT _____

SETUP
_____
_____
_____

A/B/C GRADE TRADE   RANDOM TRADE?

STOP ADHERED TO Y/N

IF NOT WHY NOT?
_____
_____
_____

TAKE PROFIT ADHERED TO Y/N

IF NOT WHY NOT?
_____
_____
_____

BREAK EVEN ADHERED TO Y/N

IF NOT WHY NOT?
_____
_____
_____

LESSONS I LEARNED FROM THIS TRADE

_____
_____
_____
_____
_____
_____

WIN/LOSS _____

PROFIT % ON ACCOUNT _____

LOSS % ON ACCOUNT _____

HOW WILL I IMPROVE ON MY NEXT TRADE

_____
_____
_____

VISUAL EXCERCISE (5-10 MINUTES)

PUT ON SOME SOFT MUSIC, LAY BACK AND RELAX AND RECREATE THE TRADE IN YOUR MIND'S EYE.

NOW SEE YOURSELF GOING THROUGH A TRADE BUT NOW YOU ARE IMPLEMENTING THE NEW LESSONS LEARNED FROM THIS TRADE. REPEAT UNTIL YOU AUTOMATICALLY ACT THIS WAY DURING TRADES

TRADER AFFIRMATIONS (SAY 100 TIMES A DAY)

I AM A GREAT TRADER/ I LEARN LESSONS FROM EVERY TRADE AND IMPLEMENT THEM/ I AM A CONSTANTLY IMPROVING TRADER/ I AIM FOR EXCELLENCE IN EVERY TRADE.

DATE _____   TIME _____

DEMO/REAL   INSTRUMENT _____

SETUP
_____
_____
_____

A/B/C GRADE TRADE   RANDOM TRADE?
  STOP ADHERED TO Y/N
  IF NOT WHY NOT?
_____
_____
_____

TAKE PROFIT ADHERED TO Y/N
IF NOT WHY NOT?
_____
_____
_____

BREAK EVEN ADHERED TO Y/N
IF NOT WHY NOT?
_____
_____
_____

LESSONS I LEARNED FROM THIS TRADE

_____
_____
_____
_____
_____

WIN/LOSS _____
PROFIT % ON ACCOUNT _____
LOSS % ON ACCOUNT _____

HOW WILL I IMPROVE ON MY NEXT TRADE
_____
_____
_____

VISUAL EXCERCISE (5-10 MINUTES)

PUT ON SOME SOFT MUSIC, LAY BACK AND RELAX AND RECREATE THE TRADE IN YOUR MIND'S EYE.
NOW SEE YOURSELF GOING THROUGH A TRADE BUT NOW YOU ARE IMPLEMENTING THE NEW LESSONS LEARNED FROM THIS TRADE. REPEAT UNTIL YOU AUTOMATICALLY ACT THIS WAY DURING TRADES

TRADER AFFIRMATIONS (SAY 100 TIMES A DAY)

I AM A GREAT TRADER/ I LEARN LESSONS FROM EVERY TRADE AND IMPLEMENT THEM/ I AM A CONSTANTLY IMPROVING TRADER/ I AIM FOR EXCELLENCE IN EVERY TRADE.

DATE _____ TIME _____

DEMO/REAL   INSTRUMENT _____

SETUP
_____
_____
_____

A/B/C GRADE TRADE   RANDOM TRADE?
STOP ADHERED TO Y/N
IF NOT WHY NOT?
_____
_____
_____

TAKE PROFIT ADHERED TO Y/N
IF NOT WHY NOT?
_____
_____
_____

BREAK EVEN ADHERED TO Y/N
IF NOT WHY NOT?
_____
_____
_____

LESSONS I LEARNED FROM THIS TRADE

_____
_____
_____
_____
_____
_____

WIN/LOSS _____

PROFIT % ON ACCOUNT _____

LOSS % ON ACCOUNT _____

HOW WILL I IMPROVE ON MY NEXT TRADE

_____
_____
_____

VISUAL EXCERCISE (5-10 MINUTES)

PUT ON SOME SOFT MUSIC, LAY BACK AND RELAX AND RECREATE THE TRADE IN YOUR MIND'S EYE.

NOW SEE YOURSELF GOING THROUGH A TRADE BUT NOW YOU ARE IMPLEMENTING THE NEW LESSONS LEARNED FROM THIS TRADE. REPEAT UNTIL YOU AUTOMATICALLY ACT THIS WAY DURING TRADES

TRADER AFFIRMATIONS (SAY 100 TIMES A DAY)

I AM A GREAT TRADER/ I LEARN LESSONS FROM EVERY TRADE AND IMPLEMENT THEM/ I AM A CONSTANTLY IMPROVING TRADER/ I AIM FOR EXCELLENCE IN EVERY TRADE.

DATE _____ TIME _____

DEMO/REAL   INSTRUMENT _____

SETUP
_____
_____
_____

A/B/C GRADE TRADE   RANDOM TRADE?
STOP ADHERED TO Y/N
IF NOT WHY NOT?
_____
_____
_____

TAKE PROFIT ADHERED TO Y/N
IF NOT WHY NOT?
_____
_____
_____

BREAK EVEN ADHERED TO Y/N
IF NOT WHY NOT?
_____
_____
_____

LESSONS I LEARNED FROM THIS TRADE

_____
_____
_____
_____
_____
_____

WIN/LOSS _____
PROFIT % ON ACCOUNT _____
LOSS % ON ACCOUNT _____

HOW WILL I IMPROVE ON MY NEXT TRADE

_____
_____
_____

VISUAL EXCERCISE (5-10 MINUTES)

PUT ON SOME SOFT MUSIC, LAY BACK AND RELAX AND RECREATE THE TRADE IN YOUR MIND'S EYE.

NOW SEE YOURSELF GOING THROUGH A TRADE BUT NOW YOU ARE IMPLEMENTING THE NEW LESSONS LEARNED FROM THIS TRADE. REPEAT UNTIL YOU AUTOMATICALLY ACT THIS WAY DURING TRADES

TRADER AFFIRMATIONS (SAY 100 TIMES A DAY)

I AM A GREAT TRADER/ I LEARN LESSONS FROM EVERY TRADE AND IMPLEMENT THEM/ I AM A CONSTANTLY IMPROVING TRADER/ I AIM FOR EXCELLENCE IN EVERY TRADE.

DATE _____   TIME _____

DEMO/REAL   INSTRUMENT _____

SETUP
_____
_____
_____

A/B/C GRADE TRADE   RANDOM TRADE?
STOP ADHERED TO Y/N
IF NOT WHY NOT?
_____
_____
_____

TAKE PROFIT ADHERED TO Y/N
IF NOT WHY NOT?
_____
_____
_____

BREAK EVEN ADHERED TO Y/N
IF NOT WHY NOT?
_____
_____
_____

LESSONS I LEARNED FROM THIS TRADE

_____
_____
_____
_____
_____

WIN/LOSS _____

PROFIT % ON ACCOUNT _____

LOSS % ON ACCOUNT _____

HOW WILL I IMPROVE ON MY NEXT TRADE

_____
_____
_____

VISUAL EXCERCISE (5-10 MINUTES)

PUT ON SOME SOFT MUSIC, LAY BACK AND RELAX AND RECREATE THE TRADE IN YOUR MIND'S EYE.

NOW SEE YOURSELF GOING THROUGH A TRADE BUT NOW YOU ARE IMPLEMENTING THE NEW LESSONS LEARNED FROM THIS TRADE. REPEAT UNTIL YOU AUTOMATICALLY ACT THIS WAY DURING TRADES

TRADER AFFIRMATIONS (SAY 100 TIMES A DAY)

I AM A GREAT TRADER/ I LEARN LESSONS FROM EVERY TRADE AND IMPLEMENT THEM/ I AM A CONSTANTLY IMPROVING TRADER/ I AIM FOR EXCELLENCE IN EVERY TRADE.

DATE _____ TIME _____

DEMO/REAL   INSTRUMENT _____

SETUP
_____
_____
_____

A/B/C GRADE TRADE   RANDOM TRADE?

  STOP ADHERED TO Y/N

  IF NOT WHY NOT?
_____
_____
_____

TAKE PROFIT ADHERED TO Y/N

IF NOT WHY NOT?
_____
_____
_____

BREAK EVEN ADHERED TO Y/N

IF NOT WHY NOT?
_____
_____
_____

LESSONS I LEARNED FROM THIS TRADE

_____
_____
_____
_____
_____

WIN/LOSS _____

PROFIT % ON ACCOUNT _____

LOSS % ON ACCOUNT _____

HOW WILL I IMPROVE ON MY NEXT TRADE
_____
_____
_____

VISUAL EXCERCISE (5-10 MINUTES)

PUT ON SOME SOFT MUSIC, LAY BACK AND RELAX AND RECREATE THE TRADE IN YOUR MIND'S EYE.

NOW SEE YOURSELF GOING THROUGH A TRADE BUT NOW YOU ARE IMPLEMENTING THE NEW LESSONS LEARNED FROM THIS TRADE. REPEAT UNTIL YOU AUTOMATICALLY ACT THIS WAY DURING TRADES

TRADER AFFIRMATIONS (SAY 100 TIMES A DAY)

I AM A GREAT TRADER/ I LEARN LESSONS FROM EVERY TRADE AND IMPLEMENT THEM/ I AM A CONSTANTLY IMPROVING TRADER/ I AIM FOR EXCELLENCE IN EVERY TRADE.

DATE _____   TIME _____

DEMO/REAL   INSTRUMENT _____

SETUP
_____
_____
_____

A/B/C GRADE TRADE   RANDOM TRADE?

STOP ADHERED TO Y/N

IF NOT WHY NOT?
_____
_____
_____

TAKE PROFIT ADHERED TO Y/N

IF NOT WHY NOT?
_____
_____
_____

BREAK EVEN ADHERED TO Y/N

IF NOT WHY NOT?
_____
_____
_____

LESSONS I LEARNED FROM THIS TRADE

_____
_____
_____
_____
_____

WIN/LOSS _____
PROFIT % ON ACCOUNT _____
LOSS % ON ACCOUNT _____

HOW WILL I IMPROVE ON MY NEXT TRADE
_____
_____
_____

VISUAL EXCERCISE (5-10 MINUTES)

PUT ON SOME SOFT MUSIC, LAY BACK AND RELAX AND RECREATE THE TRADE IN YOUR MIND'S EYE.
NOW SEE YOURSELF GOING THROUGH A TRADE BUT NOW YOU ARE IMPLEMENTING THE NEW LESSONS LEARNED FROM THIS TRADE. REPEAT UNTIL YOU AUTOMATICALLY ACT THIS WAY DURING TRADES

TRADER AFFIRMATIONS (SAY 100 TIMES A DAY)

I AM A GREAT TRADER/ I LEARN LESSONS FROM EVERY TRADE AND IMPLEMENT THEM/ I AM A CONSTANTLY IMPROVING TRADER/ I AIM FOR EXCELLENCE IN EVERY TRADE.

DATE _____   TIME _____

DEMO/REAL   INSTRUMENT _____

SETUP
_____
_____
_____

A/B/C GRADE TRADE   RANDOM TRADE?

STOP ADHERED TO Y/N

IF NOT WHY NOT?
_____
_____
_____

TAKE PROFIT ADHERED TO Y/N

IF NOT WHY NOT?
_____
_____
_____

BREAK EVEN ADHERED TO Y/N

IF NOT WHY NOT?
_____
_____
_____

LESSONS I LEARNED FROM THIS TRADE

_____
_____
_____
_____
_____
_____

WIN/LOSS _____

PROFIT % ON ACCOUNT _____

LOSS % ON ACCOUNT _____

HOW WILL I IMPROVE ON MY NEXT TRADE

_____
_____
_____

VISUAL EXCERCISE (5-10 MINUTES)

PUT ON SOME SOFT MUSIC, LAY BACK AND RELAX AND RECREATE THE TRADE IN YOUR MIND'S EYE.

NOW SEE YOURSELF GOING THROUGH A TRADE BUT NOW YOU ARE IMPLEMENTING THE NEW LESSONS LEARNED FROM THIS TRADE. REPEAT UNTIL YOU AUTOMATICALLY ACT THIS WAY DURING TRADES

TRADER AFFIRMATIONS (SAY 100 TIMES A DAY)

I AM A GREAT TRADER/ I LEARN LESSONS FROM EVERY TRADE AND IMPLEMENT THEM/ I AM A CONSTANTLY IMPROVING TRADER/ I AIM FOR EXCELLENCE IN EVERY TRADE.

DATE _____   TIME _____

DEMO/REAL   INSTRUMENT _____

SETUP
_____
_____
_____

A/B/C GRADE TRADE   RANDOM TRADE?

STOP ADHERED TO Y/N

IF NOT WHY NOT?
_____
_____
_____

TAKE PROFIT ADHERED TO Y/N

IF NOT WHY NOT?
_____
_____
_____

BREAK EVEN ADHERED TO Y/N

IF NOT WHY NOT?
_____
_____
_____

LESSONS I LEARNED FROM THIS TRADE

_____
_____
_____
_____
_____

WIN/LOSS _____
PROFIT % ON ACCOUNT _____
LOSS % ON ACCOUNT _____

HOW WILL I IMPROVE ON MY NEXT TRADE

_____
_____
_____

VISUAL EXCERCISE (5-10 MINUTES)

PUT ON SOME SOFT MUSIC, LAY BACK AND RELAX AND RECREATE THE TRADE IN YOUR MIND'S EYE.

NOW SEE YOURSELF GOING THROUGH A TRADE BUT NOW YOU ARE IMPLEMENTING THE NEW LESSONS LEARNED FROM THIS TRADE. REPEAT UNTIL YOU AUTOMATICALLY ACT THIS WAY DURING TRADES

TRADER AFFIRMATIONS (SAY 100 TIMES A DAY)

I AM A GREAT TRADER/ I LEARN LESSONS FROM EVERY TRADE AND IMPLEMENT THEM/ I AM A CONSTANTLY IMPROVING TRADER/ I AIM FOR EXCELLENCE IN EVERY TRADE.

DATE _____ TIME _____

DEMO/REAL   INSTRUMENT _____

SETUP
_____
_____
_____

A/B/C GRADE TRADE   RANDOM TRADE?
  STOP ADHERED TO Y/N
  IF NOT WHY NOT?
_____
_____
_____

TAKE PROFIT ADHERED TO Y/N
IF NOT WHY NOT?
_____
_____
_____

BREAK EVEN ADHERED TO Y/N
IF NOT WHY NOT?
_____
_____
_____

LESSONS I LEARNED FROM THIS TRADE

_____
_____
_____
_____
_____
_____

WIN/LOSS _____

PROFIT % ON ACCOUNT _____

LOSS % ON ACCOUNT _____

HOW WILL I IMPROVE ON MY NEXT TRADE

_____
_____
_____

VISUAL EXCERCISE (5-10 MINUTES)

PUT ON SOME SOFT MUSIC, LAY BACK AND RELAX AND RECREATE THE TRADE IN YOUR MIND'S EYE.

NOW SEE YOURSELF GOING THROUGH A TRADE BUT NOW YOU ARE IMPLEMENTING THE NEW LESSONS LEARNED FROM THIS TRADE. REPEAT UNTIL YOU AUTOMATICALLY ACT THIS WAY DURING TRADES

TRADER AFFIRMATIONS (SAY 100 TIMES A DAY)

I AM A GREAT TRADER/ I LEARN LESSONS FROM EVERY TRADE AND IMPLEMENT THEM/ I AM A CONSTANTLY IMPROVING TRADER/ I AIM FOR EXCELLENCE IN EVERY TRADE.

DATE _____   TIME _____

DEMO/REAL   INSTRUMENT _____

SETUP
_____
_____
_____

A/B/C GRADE TRADE   RANDOM TRADE?

STOP ADHERED TO Y/N

IF NOT WHY NOT?
_____
_____
_____

TAKE PROFIT ADHERED TO Y/N

IF NOT WHY NOT?
_____
_____
_____

BREAK EVEN ADHERED TO Y/N

IF NOT WHY NOT?
_____
_____
_____

LESSONS I LEARNED FROM THIS TRADE

_____
_____
_____
_____
_____
_____

WIN/LOSS _____
PROFIT % ON ACCOUNT _____
LOSS % ON ACCOUNT _____

HOW WILL I IMPROVE ON MY NEXT TRADE

_____
_____
_____

VISUAL EXCERCISE (5-10 MINUTES)

PUT ON SOME SOFT MUSIC, LAY BACK AND RELAX AND RECREATE THE TRADE IN YOUR MIND'S EYE.

NOW SEE YOURSELF GOING THROUGH A TRADE BUT NOW YOU ARE IMPLEMENTING THE NEW LESSONS LEARNED FROM THIS TRADE. REPEAT UNTIL YOU AUTOMATICALLY ACT THIS WAY DURING TRADES

TRADER AFFIRMATIONS (SAY 100 TIMES A DAY)

I AM A GREAT TRADER/ I LEARN LESSONS FROM EVERY TRADE AND IMPLEMENT THEM/ I AM A CONSTANTLY IMPROVING TRADER/ I AIM FOR EXCELLENCE IN EVERY TRADE.

DATE _____ TIME _____

DEMO/REAL   INSTRUMENT _____

SETUP
_____
_____
_____

A/B/C GRADE TRADE   RANDOM TRADE?
STOP ADHERED TO Y/N
IF NOT WHY NOT?
_____
_____
_____

TAKE PROFIT ADHERED TO Y/N
IF NOT WHY NOT?
_____
_____
_____

BREAK EVEN ADHERED TO Y/N
IF NOT WHY NOT?
_____
_____
_____

LESSONS I LEARNED FROM THIS TRADE

_____
_____
_____
_____
_____
_____

WIN/LOSS _____
PROFIT % ON ACCOUNT _____
LOSS % ON ACCOUNT _____

HOW WILL I IMPROVE ON MY NEXT TRADE
_____
_____
_____

VISUAL EXCERCISE (5-10 MINUTES)

PUT ON SOME SOFT MUSIC, LAY BACK AND RELAX AND RECREATE THE TRADE IN YOUR MIND'S EYE.
NOW SEE YOURSELF GOING THROUGH A TRADE BUT NOW YOU ARE IMPLEMENTING THE NEW LESSONS LEARNED FROM THIS TRADE. REPEAT UNTIL YOU AUTOMATICALLY ACT THIS WAY DURING TRADES

TRADER AFFIRMATIONS (SAY 100 TIMES A DAY)

I AM A GREAT TRADER/ I LEARN LESSONS FROM EVERY TRADE AND IMPLEMENT THEM/ I AM A CONSTANTLY IMPROVING TRADER/ I AIM FOR EXCELLENCE IN EVERY TRADE.

DATE _____   TIME _____

DEMO/REAL   INSTRUMENT _____

SETUP
_____
_____
_____

A/B/C GRADE TRADE   RANDOM TRADE?
STOP ADHERED TO Y/N
IF NOT WHY NOT?
_____
_____
_____

TAKE PROFIT ADHERED TO Y/N
IF NOT WHY NOT?
_____
_____
_____

BREAK EVEN ADHERED TO Y/N
IF NOT WHY NOT?
_____
_____
_____

LESSONS I LEARNED FROM THIS TRADE

_____
_____
_____
_____
_____
_____

WIN/LOSS _____

PROFIT % ON ACCOUNT _____

LOSS % ON ACCOUNT _____

HOW WILL I IMPROVE ON MY NEXT TRADE

_____
_____
_____

VISUAL EXCERCISE (5-10 MINUTES)

PUT ON SOME SOFT MUSIC, LAY BACK AND RELAX AND RECREATE THE TRADE IN YOUR MIND'S EYE.

NOW SEE YOURSELF GOING THROUGH A TRADE BUT NOW YOU ARE IMPLEMENTING THE NEW LESSONS LEARNED FROM THIS TRADE. REPEAT UNTIL YOU AUTOMATICALLY ACT THIS WAY DURING TRADES

TRADER AFFIRMATIONS (SAY 100 TIMES A DAY)

I AM A GREAT TRADER/ I LEARN LESSONS FROM EVERY TRADE AND IMPLEMENT THEM/ I AM A CONSTANTLY IMPROVING TRADER/ I AIM FOR EXCELLENCE IN EVERY TRADE.

DATE _____ TIME _____

DEMO/REAL   INSTRUMENT _____

SETUP
_____
_____
_____

A/B/C GRADE TRADE   RANDOM TRADE?
STOP ADHERED TO Y/N
IF NOT WHY NOT?
_____
_____
_____

TAKE PROFIT ADHERED TO Y/N
IF NOT WHY NOT?
_____
_____
_____

BREAK EVEN ADHERED TO Y/N
IF NOT WHY NOT?
_____
_____
_____

LESSONS I LEARNED FROM THIS TRADE

_____
_____
_____
_____
_____
_____

WIN/LOSS _____

PROFIT % ON ACCOUNT _____

LOSS % ON ACCOUNT _____

HOW WILL I IMPROVE ON MY NEXT TRADE

_____
_____
_____

VISUAL EXCERCISE (5-10 MINUTES)

PUT ON SOME SOFT MUSIC, LAY BACK AND RELAX AND RECREATE THE TRADE IN YOUR MIND'S EYE.

NOW SEE YOURSELF GOING THROUGH A TRADE BUT NOW YOU ARE IMPLEMENTING THE NEW LESSONS LEARNED FROM THIS TRADE. REPEAT UNTIL YOU AUTOMATICALLY ACT THIS WAY DURING TRADES

TRADER AFFIRMATIONS (SAY 100 TIMES A DAY)

I AM A GREAT TRADER/ I LEARN LESSONS FROM EVERY TRADE AND IMPLEMENT THEM/ I AM A CONSTANTLY IMPROVING TRADER/ I AIM FOR EXCELLENCE IN EVERY TRADE.

DATE _____ TIME _____

DEMO/REAL   INSTRUMENT _____

SETUP
_____
_____
_____

A/B/C GRADE TRADE   RANDOM TRADE?
  STOP ADHERED TO Y/N
  IF NOT WHY NOT?
_____
_____
_____

TAKE PROFIT ADHERED TO Y/N
IF NOT WHY NOT?
_____
_____
_____

BREAK EVEN ADHERED TO Y/N
IF NOT WHY NOT?
_____
_____
_____

LESSONS I LEARNED FROM THIS TRADE

_____
_____
_____
_____
_____
_____

WIN/LOSS _____

PROFIT % ON ACCOUNT _____

LOSS % ON ACCOUNT _____

HOW WILL I IMPROVE ON MY NEXT TRADE

_____
_____
_____

VISUAL EXCERCISE (5-10 MINUTES)

PUT ON SOME SOFT MUSIC, LAY BACK AND RELAX AND RECREATE THE TRADE IN YOUR MIND'S EYE.

NOW SEE YOURSELF GOING THROUGH A TRADE BUT NOW YOU ARE IMPLEMENTING THE NEW LESSONS LEARNED FROM THIS TRADE. REPEAT UNTIL YOU AUTOMATICALLY ACT THIS WAY DURING TRADES

TRADER AFFIRMATIONS (SAY 100 TIMES A DAY)

I AM A GREAT TRADER/ I LEARN LESSONS FROM EVERY TRADE AND IMPLEMENT THEM/ I AM A CONSTANTLY IMPROVING TRADER/ I AIM FOR EXCELLENCE IN EVERY TRADE.

DATE _____ TIME _____

DEMO/REAL   INSTRUMENT _____

SETUP
_____
_____

A/B/C GRADE TRADE   RANDOM TRADE?

STOP ADHERED TO Y/N

IF NOT WHY NOT?
_____
_____
_____

TAKE PROFIT ADHERED TO Y/N

IF NOT WHY NOT?
_____
_____
_____

BREAK EVEN ADHERED TO Y/N

IF NOT WHY NOT?
_____
_____
_____

LESSONS I LEARNED FROM THIS TRADE

_____
_____
_____
_____
_____
_____

WIN/LOSS _____

PROFIT % ON ACCOUNT _____

LOSS % ON ACCOUNT _____

HOW WILL I IMPROVE ON MY NEXT TRADE
_____
_____
_____

VISUAL EXCERCISE (5-10 MINUTES)

PUT ON SOME SOFT MUSIC, LAY BACK AND RELAX AND RECREATE THE TRADE IN YOUR MIND'S EYE.

NOW SEE YOURSELF GOING THROUGH A TRADE BUT NOW YOU ARE IMPLEMENTING THE NEW LESSONS LEARNED FROM THIS TRADE. REPEAT UNTIL YOU AUTOMATICALLY ACT THIS WAY DURING TRADES

TRADER AFFIRMATIONS (SAY 100 TIMES A DAY)

I AM A GREAT TRADER/ I LEARN LESSONS FROM EVERY TRADE AND IMPLEMENT THEM/ I AM A CONSTANTLY IMPROVING TRADER/ I AIM FOR EXCELLENCE IN EVERY TRADE.

DATE _____   TIME _____

DEMO/REAL   INSTRUMENT _____

SETUP
_____
_____
_____

A/B/C GRADE TRADE   RANDOM TRADE?
STOP ADHERED TO Y/N
IF NOT WHY NOT?
_____
_____
_____

TAKE PROFIT ADHERED TO Y/N
IF NOT WHY NOT?
_____
_____
_____

BREAK EVEN ADHERED TO Y/N
IF NOT WHY NOT?
_____
_____
_____

LESSONS I LEARNED FROM THIS TRADE

_____
_____
_____
_____
_____
_____

WIN/LOSS _____
PROFIT % ON ACCOUNT _____
LOSS % ON ACCOUNT _____

HOW WILL I IMPROVE ON MY NEXT TRADE
_____
_____
_____

VISUAL EXCERCISE (5-10 MINUTES)

PUT ON SOME SOFT MUSIC, LAY BACK AND RELAX AND RECREATE THE TRADE IN YOUR MIND'S EYE.
NOW SEE YOURSELF GOING THROUGH A TRADE BUT NOW YOU ARE IMPLEMENTING THE NEW LESSONS LEARNED FROM THIS TRADE. REPEAT UNTIL YOU AUTOMATICALLY ACT THIS WAY DURING TRADES

TRADER AFFIRMATIONS (SAY 100 TIMES A DAY)

I AM A GREAT TRADER/ I LEARN LESSONS FROM EVERY TRADE AND IMPLEMENT THEM/ I AM A CONSTANTLY IMPROVING TRADER/ I AIM FOR EXCELLENCE IN EVERY TRADE.

DATE _____ TIME _____

DEMO/REAL   INSTRUMENT _____

SETUP
_____
_____
_____

A/B/C GRADE TRADE   RANDOM TRADE?

STOP ADHERED TO Y/N

IF NOT WHY NOT?
_____
_____
_____

TAKE PROFIT ADHERED TO Y/N

IF NOT WHY NOT?
_____
_____
_____

BREAK EVEN ADHERED TO Y/N

IF NOT WHY NOT?
_____
_____
_____

LESSONS I LEARNED FROM THIS TRADE

_____
_____
_____
_____
_____
_____

WIN/LOSS _____
PROFIT % ON ACCOUNT _____
LOSS % ON ACCOUNT _____

HOW WILL I IMPROVE ON MY NEXT TRADE

_____
_____
_____

VISUAL EXCERCISE (5-10 MINUTES)

PUT ON SOME SOFT MUSIC, LAY BACK AND RELAX AND RECREATE THE TRADE IN YOUR MIND'S EYE.

NOW SEE YOURSELF GOING THROUGH A TRADE BUT NOW YOU ARE IMPLEMENTING THE NEW LESSONS LEARNED FROM THIS TRADE. REPEAT UNTIL YOU AUTOMATICALLY ACT THIS WAY DURING TRADES

TRADER AFFIRMATIONS (SAY 100 TIMES A DAY)

I AM A GREAT TRADER/ I LEARN LESSONS FROM EVERY TRADE AND IMPLEMENT THEM/ I AM A CONSTANTLY IMPROVING TRADER/ I AIM FOR EXCELLENCE IN EVERY TRADE.

DATE _____ TIME _____

DEMO/REAL   INSTRUMENT _____

SETUP
_____
_____
_____

A/B/C GRADE TRADE   RANDOM TRADE?
  STOP ADHERED TO Y/N
  IF NOT WHY NOT?
_____
_____
_____

TAKE PROFIT ADHERED TO Y/N
IF NOT WHY NOT?
_____
_____
_____

BREAK EVEN ADHERED TO Y/N
IF NOT WHY NOT?
_____
_____
_____

LESSONS I LEARNED FROM THIS TRADE

_____
_____
_____
_____
_____
_____

WIN/LOSS _____

PROFIT % ON ACCOUNT _____

LOSS % ON ACCOUNT _____

HOW WILL I IMPROVE ON MY NEXT TRADE

_____
_____
_____

VISUAL EXCERCISE (5-10 MINUTES)

PUT ON SOME SOFT MUSIC, LAY BACK AND RELAX AND RECREATE THE TRADE IN YOUR MIND'S EYE.

NOW SEE YOURSELF GOING THROUGH A TRADE BUT NOW YOU ARE IMPLEMENTING THE NEW LESSONS LEARNED FROM THIS TRADE. REPEAT UNTIL YOU AUTOMATICALLY ACT THIS WAY DURING TRADES

TRADER AFFIRMATIONS (SAY 100 TIMES A DAY)

I AM A GREAT TRADER/ I LEARN LESSONS FROM EVERY TRADE AND IMPLEMENT THEM/ I AM A CONSTANTLY IMPROVING TRADER/ I AIM FOR EXCELLENCE IN EVERY TRADE.

DATE _____ TIME _____

DEMO/REAL   INSTRUMENT _____

SETUP
_____
_____
_____

A/B/C GRADE TRADE   RANDOM TRADE?

STOP ADHERED TO Y/N

IF NOT WHY NOT?
_____
_____
_____

TAKE PROFIT ADHERED TO Y/N

IF NOT WHY NOT?
_____
_____
_____

BREAK EVEN ADHERED TO Y/N

IF NOT WHY NOT?
_____
_____
_____

LESSONS I LEARNED FROM THIS TRADE

_____
_____
_____
_____
_____

WIN/LOSS _____
PROFIT % ON ACCOUNT _____
LOSS % ON ACCOUNT _____

HOW WILL I IMPROVE ON MY NEXT TRADE
_____
_____
_____

VISUAL EXCERCISE (5-10 MINUTES)

PUT ON SOME SOFT MUSIC, LAY BACK AND RELAX AND RECREATE THE TRADE IN YOUR MIND'S EYE.
NOW SEE YOURSELF GOING THROUGH A TRADE BUT NOW YOU ARE IMPLEMENTING THE NEW LESSONS LEARNED FROM THIS TRADE. REPEAT UNTIL YOU AUTOMATICALLY ACT THIS WAY DURING TRADES

TRADER AFFIRMATIONS (SAY 100 TIMES A DAY)

I AM A GREAT TRADER/ I LEARN LESSONS FROM EVERY TRADE AND IMPLEMENT THEM/ I AM A CONSTANTLY IMPROVING TRADER/ I AIM FOR EXCELLENCE IN EVERY TRADE.

DATE _____ TIME _____

DEMO/REAL   INSTRUMENT _____

SETUP
_____
_____
_____

A/B/C GRADE TRADE   RANDOM TRADE?

STOP ADHERED TO Y/N

IF NOT WHY NOT?
_____
_____
_____

TAKE PROFIT ADHERED TO Y/N

IF NOT WHY NOT?
_____
_____
_____

BREAK EVEN ADHERED TO Y/N

IF NOT WHY NOT?
_____
_____
_____

LESSONS I LEARNED FROM THIS TRADE

_____
_____
_____
_____
_____
_____

WIN/LOSS _____
PROFIT % ON ACCOUNT _____
LOSS % ON ACCOUNT _____

HOW WILL I IMPROVE ON MY NEXT TRADE
_____
_____
_____

VISUAL EXCERCISE (5-10 MINUTES)

PUT ON SOME SOFT MUSIC, LAY BACK AND RELAX AND RECREATE THE TRADE IN YOUR MIND'S EYE.

NOW SEE YOURSELF GOING THROUGH A TRADE BUT NOW YOU ARE IMPLEMENTING THE NEW LESSONS LEARNED FROM THIS TRADE. REPEAT UNTIL YOU AUTOMATICALLY ACT THIS WAY DURING TRADES

TRADER AFFIRMATIONS (SAY 100 TIMES A DAY)

I AM A GREAT TRADER/ I LEARN LESSONS FROM EVERY TRADE AND IMPLEMENT THEM/ I AM A CONSTANTLY IMPROVING TRADER/ I AIM FOR EXCELLENCE IN EVERY TRADE.

DATE _____ TIME _____

DEMO/REAL   INSTRUMENT _____

SETUP
_____
_____
_____

A/B/C GRADE TRADE   RANDOM TRADE?

STOP ADHERED TO Y/N

IF NOT WHY NOT?
_____
_____
_____

TAKE PROFIT ADHERED TO Y/N

IF NOT WHY NOT?
_____
_____
_____

BREAK EVEN ADHERED TO Y/N

IF NOT WHY NOT?
_____
_____
_____

LESSONS I LEARNED FROM THIS TRADE

_____
_____
_____
_____
_____
_____

WIN/LOSS _____
PROFIT % ON ACCOUNT _____
LOSS % ON ACCOUNT _____

HOW WILL I IMPROVE ON MY NEXT TRADE

_____
_____
_____

VISUAL EXCERCISE (5-10 MINUTES)

PUT ON SOME SOFT MUSIC, LAY BACK AND RELAX AND RECREATE THE TRADE IN YOUR MIND'S EYE.

NOW SEE YOURSELF GOING THROUGH A TRADE BUT NOW YOU ARE IMPLEMENTING THE NEW LESSONS LEARNED FROM THIS TRADE. REPEAT UNTIL YOU AUTOMATICALLY ACT THIS WAY DURING TRADES

TRADER AFFIRMATIONS (SAY 100 TIMES A DAY)

I AM A GREAT TRADER/ I LEARN LESSONS FROM EVERY TRADE AND IMPLEMENT THEM/ I AM A CONSTANTLY IMPROVING TRADER/ I AIM FOR EXCELLENCE IN EVERY TRADE.

DATE _____ TIME _____

DEMO/REAL   INSTRUMENT _____

SETUP
_____
_____

_____

A/B/C GRADE TRADE   RANDOM TRADE?
STOP ADHERED TO Y/N
IF NOT WHY NOT?
_____
_____
_____

TAKE PROFIT ADHERED TO Y/N
IF NOT WHY NOT?
_____
_____
_____

BREAK EVEN ADHERED TO Y/N
IF NOT WHY NOT?
_____
_____
_____

LESSONS I LEARNED FROM THIS TRADE

_____
_____
_____
_____
_____
_____

WIN/LOSS _____
PROFIT % ON ACCOUNT _____
LOSS % ON ACCOUNT _____

HOW WILL I IMPROVE ON MY NEXT TRADE

_____
_____
_____

VISUAL EXCERCISE (5-10 MINUTES)

PUT ON SOME SOFT MUSIC, LAY BACK AND RELAX AND RECREATE THE TRADE IN YOUR MIND'S EYE.
NOW SEE YOURSELF GOING THROUGH A TRADE BUT NOW YOU ARE IMPLEMENTING THE NEW LESSONS LEARNED FROM THIS TRADE. REPEAT UNTIL YOU AUTOMATICALLY ACT THIS WAY DURING TRADES

TRADER AFFIRMATIONS (SAY 100 TIMES A DAY)

I AM A GREAT TRADER/ I LEARN LESSONS FROM EVERY TRADE AND IMPLEMENT THEM/ I AM A CONSTANTLY IMPROVING TRADER/ I AIM FOR EXCELLENCE IN EVERY TRADE.

DATE _____   TIME _____

DEMO/REAL   INSTRUMENT _____

SETUP
_____
_____
_____

A/B/C GRADE TRADE   RANDOM TRADE?

STOP ADHERED TO Y/N

IF NOT WHY NOT?
_____
_____
_____

TAKE PROFIT ADHERED TO Y/N

IF NOT WHY NOT?
_____
_____
_____

BREAK EVEN ADHERED TO Y/N

IF NOT WHY NOT?
_____
_____
_____

LESSONS I LEARNED FROM THIS TRADE
_____
_____
_____
_____
_____

WIN/LOSS _____
PROFIT % ON ACCOUNT _____
LOSS % ON ACCOUNT _____

HOW WILL I IMPROVE ON MY NEXT TRADE
_____
_____
_____

VISUAL EXCERCISE (5-10 MINUTES)

PUT ON SOME SOFT MUSIC, LAY BACK AND RELAX AND RECREATE THE TRADE IN YOUR MIND'S EYE.
NOW SEE YOURSELF GOING THROUGH A TRADE BUT NOW YOU ARE IMPLEMENTING THE NEW LESSONS LEARNED FROM THIS TRADE. REPEAT UNTIL YOU AUTOMATICALLY ACT THIS WAY DURING TRADES

TRADER AFFIRMATIONS (SAY 100 TIMES A DAY)

I AM A GREAT TRADER/ I LEARN LESSONS FROM EVERY TRADE AND IMPLEMENT THEM/ I AM A CONSTANTLY IMPROVING TRADER/ I AIM FOR EXCELLENCE IN EVERY TRADE.

DATE _____ TIME _____

DEMO/REAL   INSTRUMENT _____

SETUP
_____
_____
_____

A/B/C GRADE TRADE   RANDOM TRADE?

STOP ADHERED TO Y/N

IF NOT WHY NOT?
_____
_____
_____

TAKE PROFIT ADHERED TO Y/N

IF NOT WHY NOT?
_____
_____
_____

BREAK EVEN ADHERED TO Y/N

IF NOT WHY NOT?
_____
_____
_____

LESSONS I LEARNED FROM THIS TRADE

_____
_____
_____
_____
_____
_____

WIN/LOSS _____

PROFIT % ON ACCOUNT _____

LOSS % ON ACCOUNT _____

HOW WILL I IMPROVE ON MY NEXT TRADE

_____
_____
_____

VISUAL EXCERCISE (5-10 MINUTES)

PUT ON SOME SOFT MUSIC, LAY BACK AND RELAX AND RECREATE THE TRADE IN YOUR MIND'S EYE.

NOW SEE YOURSELF GOING THROUGH A TRADE BUT NOW YOU ARE IMPLEMENTING THE NEW LESSONS LEARNED FROM THIS TRADE. REPEAT UNTIL YOU AUTOMATICALLY ACT THIS WAY DURING TRADES

TRADER AFFIRMATIONS (SAY 100 TIMES A DAY)

I AM A GREAT TRADER/ I LEARN LESSONS FROM EVERY TRADE AND IMPLEMENT THEM/ I AM A CONSTANTLY IMPROVING TRADER/ I AIM FOR EXCELLENCE IN EVERY TRADE.

DATE _____ TIME _____

DEMO/REAL   INSTRUMENT _____

SETUP
_____
_____
_____

A/B/C GRADE TRADE   RANDOM TRADE?

STOP ADHERED TO Y/N

IF NOT WHY NOT?
_____
_____
_____

TAKE PROFIT ADHERED TO Y/N

IF NOT WHY NOT?
_____
_____
_____

BREAK EVEN ADHERED TO Y/N

IF NOT WHY NOT?
_____
_____
_____

LESSONS I LEARNED FROM THIS TRADE

_____
_____
_____
_____
_____
_____

WIN/LOSS _____

PROFIT % ON ACCOUNT _____

LOSS % ON ACCOUNT _____

HOW WILL I IMPROVE ON MY NEXT TRADE

_____
_____
_____

VISUAL EXCERCISE (5-10 MINUTES)

PUT ON SOME SOFT MUSIC, LAY BACK AND RELAX AND RECREATE THE TRADE IN YOUR MIND'S EYE.
NOW SEE YOURSELF GOING THROUGH A TRADE BUT NOW YOU ARE IMPLEMENTING THE NEW LESSONS LEARNED FROM THIS TRADE. REPEAT UNTIL YOU AUTOMATICALLY ACT THIS WAY DURING TRADES

TRADER AFFIRMATIONS (SAY 100 TIMES A DAY)

I AM A GREAT TRADER/ I LEARN LESSONS FROM EVERY TRADE AND IMPLEMENT THEM/ I AM A CONSTANTLY IMPROVING TRADER/ I AIM FOR EXCELLENCE IN EVERY TRADE.

DATE _____ TIME _____

DEMO/REAL   INSTRUMENT _____

SETUP
_____
_____
_____

A/B/C GRADE TRADE   RANDOM TRADE?
STOP ADHERED TO Y/N
IF NOT WHY NOT?
_____
_____
_____

TAKE PROFIT ADHERED TO Y/N
IF NOT WHY NOT?
_____
_____
_____

BREAK EVEN ADHERED TO Y/N
IF NOT WHY NOT?
_____
_____
_____

LESSONS I LEARNED FROM THIS TRADE
_____
_____
_____
_____
_____

WIN/LOSS _____
PROFIT % ON ACCOUNT _____
LOSS % ON ACCOUNT _____

HOW WILL I IMPROVE ON MY NEXT TRADE
_____
_____
_____

VISUAL EXCERCISE (5-10 MINUTES)

PUT ON SOME SOFT MUSIC, LAY BACK AND RELAX AND RECREATE THE TRADE IN YOUR MIND'S EYE.

NOW SEE YOURSELF GOING THROUGH A TRADE BUT NOW YOU ARE IMPLEMENTING THE NEW LESSONS LEARNED FROM THIS TRADE. REPEAT UNTIL YOU AUTOMATICALLY ACT THIS WAY DURING TRADES

TRADER AFFIRMATIONS (SAY 100 TIMES A DAY)

I AM A GREAT TRADER/ I LEARN LESSONS FROM EVERY TRADE AND IMPLEMENT THEM/ I AM A CONSTANTLY IMPROVING TRADER/ I AIM FOR EXCELLENCE IN EVERY TRADE.

DATE _____ TIME _____

DEMO/REAL   INSTRUMENT _____

SETUP
_____
_____
_____

A/B/C GRADE TRADE   RANDOM TRADE?
STOP ADHERED TO Y/N
IF NOT WHY NOT?
_____
_____
_____

TAKE PROFIT ADHERED TO Y/N
IF NOT WHY NOT?
_____
_____
_____

BREAK EVEN ADHERED TO Y/N
IF NOT WHY NOT?
_____
_____
_____

LESSONS I LEARNED FROM THIS TRADE

_____
_____
_____
_____
_____
_____

WIN/LOSS _____

PROFIT % ON ACCOUNT _____

LOSS % ON ACCOUNT _____

HOW WILL I IMPROVE ON MY NEXT TRADE

_____
_____
_____

VISUAL EXCERCISE (5-10 MINUTES)

PUT ON SOME SOFT MUSIC, LAY BACK AND RELAX AND RECREATE THE TRADE IN YOUR MIND'S EYE.

NOW SEE YOURSELF GOING THROUGH A TRADE BUT NOW YOU ARE IMPLEMENTING THE NEW LESSONS LEARNED FROM THIS TRADE. REPEAT UNTIL YOU AUTOMATICALLY ACT THIS WAY DURING TRADES

TRADER AFFIRMATIONS (SAY 100 TIMES A DAY)

I AM A GREAT TRADER/ I LEARN LESSONS FROM EVERY TRADE AND IMPLEMENT THEM/ I AM A CONSTANTLY IMPROVING TRADER/ I AIM FOR EXCELLENCE IN EVERY TRADE.

DATE _____ TIME _____

DEMO/REAL   INSTRUMENT _____

SETUP
_____
_____
_____

A/B/C GRADE TRADE   RANDOM TRADE?

STOP ADHERED TO Y/N

IF NOT WHY NOT?
_____
_____
_____

TAKE PROFIT ADHERED TO Y/N

IF NOT WHY NOT?
_____
_____
_____

BREAK EVEN ADHERED TO Y/N

IF NOT WHY NOT?
_____
_____
_____

LESSONS I LEARNED FROM THIS TRADE

_____
_____
_____
_____
_____
_____

WIN/LOSS _____
PROFIT % ON ACCOUNT _____
LOSS % ON ACCOUNT _____

HOW WILL I IMPROVE ON MY NEXT TRADE

_____
_____
_____

VISUAL EXCERCISE (5-10 MINUTES)

PUT ON SOME SOFT MUSIC, LAY BACK AND RELAX AND RECREATE THE TRADE IN YOUR MIND'S EYE.

NOW SEE YOURSELF GOING THROUGH A TRADE BUT NOW YOU ARE IMPLEMENTING THE NEW LESSONS LEARNED FROM THIS TRADE. REPEAT UNTIL YOU AUTOMATICALLY ACT THIS WAY DURING TRADES

TRADER AFFIRMATIONS (SAY 100 TIMES A DAY)

I AM A GREAT TRADER/ I LEARN LESSONS FROM EVERY TRADE AND IMPLEMENT THEM/ I AM A CONSTANTLY IMPROVING TRADER/ I AIM FOR EXCELLENCE IN EVERY TRADE.

DATE _____ TIME _____

DEMO/REAL   INSTRUMENT _____

SETUP
_____
_____
_____

A/B/C GRADE TRADE   RANDOM TRADE?

STOP ADHERED TO Y/N

IF NOT WHY NOT?
_____
_____
_____

TAKE PROFIT ADHERED TO Y/N

IF NOT WHY NOT?
_____
_____
_____

BREAK EVEN ADHERED TO Y/N

IF NOT WHY NOT?
_____
_____
_____

LESSONS I LEARNED FROM THIS TRADE

_____
_____
_____
_____
_____
_____

WIN/LOSS _____
PROFIT % ON ACCOUNT _____
LOSS % ON ACCOUNT _____

HOW WILL I IMPROVE ON MY NEXT TRADE
_____
_____
_____

VISUAL EXCERCISE (5-10 MINUTES)

PUT ON SOME SOFT MUSIC, LAY BACK AND RELAX AND RECREATE THE TRADE IN YOUR MIND'S EYE.
NOW SEE YOURSELF GOING THROUGH A TRADE BUT NOW YOU ARE IMPLEMENTING THE NEW LESSONS LEARNED FROM THIS TRADE. REPEAT UNTIL YOU AUTOMATICALLY ACT THIS WAY DURING TRADES

TRADER AFFIRMATIONS (SAY 100 TIMES A DAY)

I AM A GREAT TRADER/ I LEARN LESSONS FROM EVERY TRADE AND IMPLEMENT THEM/ I AM A CONSTANTLY IMPROVING TRADER/ I AIM FOR EXCELLENCE IN EVERY TRADE.

DATE _____ TIME _____

DEMO/REAL   INSTRUMENT _____

SETUP
_____
_____
_____

A/B/C GRADE TRADE   RANDOM TRADE?
STOP ADHERED TO Y/N
IF NOT WHY NOT?
_____
_____
_____

TAKE PROFIT ADHERED TO Y/N
IF NOT WHY NOT?
_____
_____
_____

BREAK EVEN ADHERED TO Y/N
IF NOT WHY NOT?
_____
_____
_____

LESSONS I LEARNED FROM THIS TRADE

_____
_____
_____
_____
_____

WIN/LOSS _____

PROFIT % ON ACCOUNT _____

LOSS % ON ACCOUNT _____

HOW WILL I IMPROVE ON MY NEXT TRADE

_____
_____
_____

VISUAL EXCERCISE (5-10 MINUTES)

PUT ON SOME SOFT MUSIC, LAY BACK AND RELAX AND RECREATE THE TRADE IN YOUR MIND'S EYE.

NOW SEE YOURSELF GOING THROUGH A TRADE BUT NOW YOU ARE IMPLEMENTING THE NEW LESSONS LEARNED FROM THIS TRADE. REPEAT UNTIL YOU AUTOMATICALLY ACT THIS WAY DURING TRADES

TRADER AFFIRMATIONS (SAY 100 TIMES A DAY)

I AM A GREAT TRADER/ I LEARN LESSONS FROM EVERY TRADE AND IMPLEMENT THEM/ I AM A CONSTANTLY IMPROVING TRADER/ I AIM FOR EXCELLENCE IN EVERY TRADE.

DATE _____ TIME _____

DEMO/REAL   INSTRUMENT _____

SETUP
_____
_____

_____

A/B/C GRADE TRADE   RANDOM TRADE?

STOP ADHERED TO Y/N

IF NOT WHY NOT?
_____
_____

_____

TAKE PROFIT ADHERED TO Y/N

IF NOT WHY NOT?
_____
_____

_____

BREAK EVEN ADHERED TO Y/N

IF NOT WHY NOT?
_____
_____
_____

LESSONS I LEARNED FROM THIS TRADE

_____
_____
_____
_____
_____

WIN/LOSS _____
PROFIT % ON ACCOUNT _____
LOSS % ON ACCOUNT _____

HOW WILL I IMPROVE ON MY NEXT TRADE
_____
_____
_____

VISUAL EXCERCISE (5-10 MINUTES)

PUT ON SOME SOFT MUSIC, LAY BACK AND RELAX AND RECREATE THE TRADE IN YOUR MIND'S EYE.

NOW SEE YOURSELF GOING THROUGH A TRADE BUT NOW YOU ARE IMPLEMENTING THE NEW LESSONS LEARNED FROM THIS TRADE. REPEAT UNTIL YOU AUTOMATICALLY ACT THIS WAY DURING TRADES

TRADER AFFIRMATIONS (SAY 100 TIMES A DAY)

I AM A GREAT TRADER/ I LEARN LESSONS FROM EVERY TRADE AND IMPLEMENT THEM/ I AM A CONSTANTLY IMPROVING TRADER/ I AIM FOR EXCELLENCE IN EVERY TRADE.

DATE _____ TIME _____

DEMO/REAL   INSTRUMENT _____

SETUP
_____
_____
_____

A/B/C GRADE TRADE   RANDOM TRADE?
STOP ADHERED TO Y/N
IF NOT WHY NOT?
_____
_____
_____

TAKE PROFIT ADHERED TO Y/N
IF NOT WHY NOT?
_____
_____
_____

BREAK EVEN ADHERED TO Y/N
IF NOT WHY NOT?
_____
_____
_____

LESSONS I LEARNED FROM THIS TRADE

_____
_____
_____
_____
_____

WIN/LOSS _____
PROFIT % ON ACCOUNT _____
LOSS % ON ACCOUNT _____

HOW WILL I IMPROVE ON MY NEXT TRADE
_____
_____
_____

VISUAL EXCERCISE (5-10 MINUTES)

PUT ON SOME SOFT MUSIC, LAY BACK AND RELAX AND RECREATE THE TRADE IN YOUR MIND'S EYE.

NOW SEE YOURSELF GOING THROUGH A TRADE BUT NOW YOU ARE IMPLEMENTING THE NEW LESSONS LEARNED FROM THIS TRADE. REPEAT UNTIL YOU AUTOMATICALLY ACT THIS WAY DURING TRADES

TRADER AFFIRMATIONS (SAY 100 TIMES A DAY)

I AM A GREAT TRADER/ I LEARN LESSONS FROM EVERY TRADE AND IMPLEMENT THEM/ I AM A CONSTANTLY IMPROVING TRADER/ I AIM FOR EXCELLENCE IN EVERY TRADE.

DATE _____ TIME _____

DEMO/REAL   INSTRUMENT _____

SETUP
_____
_____
_____

A/B/C GRADE TRADE   RANDOM TRADE?
STOP ADHERED TO Y/N
IF NOT WHY NOT?
_____
_____
_____

TAKE PROFIT ADHERED TO Y/N
IF NOT WHY NOT?
_____
_____
_____

BREAK EVEN ADHERED TO Y/N
IF NOT WHY NOT?
_____
_____
_____

LESSONS I LEARNED FROM THIS TRADE

_____
_____
_____
_____
_____
_____

WIN/LOSS _____
PROFIT % ON ACCOUNT _____
LOSS % ON ACCOUNT _____

HOW WILL I IMPROVE ON MY NEXT TRADE
_____
_____
_____

VISUAL EXCERCISE (5-10 MINUTES)

PUT ON SOME SOFT MUSIC, LAY BACK AND RELAX AND RECREATE THE TRADE IN YOUR MIND'S EYE.

NOW SEE YOURSELF GOING THROUGH A TRADE BUT NOW YOU ARE IMPLEMENTING THE NEW LESSONS LEARNED FROM THIS TRADE. REPEAT UNTIL YOU AUTOMATICALLY ACT THIS WAY DURING TRADES

TRADER AFFIRMATIONS (SAY 100 TIMES A DAY)

I AM A GREAT TRADER/ I LEARN LESSONS FROM EVERY TRADE AND IMPLEMENT THEM/ I AM A CONSTANTLY IMPROVING TRADER/ I AIM FOR EXCELLENCE IN EVERY TRADE.

DATE _____ TIME _____

DEMO/REAL   INSTRUMENT _____

SETUP
_____
_____

A/B/C GRADE TRADE   RANDOM TRADE?
STOP ADHERED TO Y/N
IF NOT WHY NOT?
_____
_____
_____

TAKE PROFIT ADHERED TO Y/N
IF NOT WHY NOT?
_____
_____
_____

BREAK EVEN ADHERED TO Y/N
IF NOT WHY NOT?
_____
_____
_____

LESSONS I LEARNED FROM THIS TRADE

_____
_____
_____
_____
_____
_____

WIN/LOSS _____

PROFIT % ON ACCOUNT _____

LOSS % ON ACCOUNT _____

HOW WILL I IMPROVE ON MY NEXT TRADE

_____
_____
_____

VISUAL EXCERCISE (5-10 MINUTES)

PUT ON SOME SOFT MUSIC, LAY BACK AND RELAX AND RECREATE THE TRADE IN YOUR MIND'S EYE.

NOW SEE YOURSELF GOING THROUGH A TRADE BUT NOW YOU ARE IMPLEMENTING THE NEW LESSONS LEARNED FROM THIS TRADE. REPEAT UNTIL YOU AUTOMATICALLY ACT THIS WAY DURING TRADES

TRADER AFFIRMATIONS (SAY 100 TIMES A DAY)

I AM A GREAT TRADER/ I LEARN LESSONS FROM EVERY TRADE AND IMPLEMENT THEM/ I AM A CONSTANTLY IMPROVING TRADER/ I AIM FOR EXCELLENCE IN EVERY TRADE.

DATE _____ TIME _____

DEMO/REAL   INSTRUMENT _____

SETUP
_____
_____
_____

A/B/C GRADE TRADE   RANDOM TRADE?

STOP ADHERED TO Y/N

IF NOT WHY NOT?
_____
_____
_____

TAKE PROFIT ADHERED TO Y/N

IF NOT WHY NOT?
_____
_____
_____

BREAK EVEN ADHERED TO Y/N

IF NOT WHY NOT?
_____
_____
_____

LESSONS I LEARNED FROM THIS TRADE

_____
_____
_____
_____
_____
_____

WIN/LOSS _____
PROFIT % ON ACCOUNT _____
LOSS % ON ACCOUNT _____

HOW WILL I IMPROVE ON MY NEXT TRADE

_____
_____
_____

VISUAL EXCERCISE (5-10 MINUTES)

PUT ON SOME SOFT MUSIC, LAY BACK AND RELAX AND RECREATE THE TRADE IN YOUR MIND'S EYE.

NOW SEE YOURSELF GOING THROUGH A TRADE BUT NOW YOU ARE IMPLEMENTING THE NEW LESSONS LEARNED FROM THIS TRADE. REPEAT UNTIL YOU AUTOMATICALLY ACT THIS WAY DURING TRADES

TRADER AFFIRMATIONS (SAY 100 TIMES A DAY)

I AM A GREAT TRADER/ I LEARN LESSONS FROM EVERY TRADE AND IMPLEMENT THEM/ I AM A CONSTANTLY IMPROVING TRADER/ I AIM FOR EXCELLENCE IN EVERY TRADE.

DATE _____ TIME _____

DEMO/REAL   INSTRUMENT _____

SETUP
_____
_____

_____

A/B/C GRADE TRADE   RANDOM TRADE?
  STOP ADHERED TO Y/N
  IF NOT WHY NOT?

_____
_____

_____

TAKE PROFIT ADHERED TO Y/N
IF NOT WHY NOT?

_____
_____

_____

BREAK EVEN ADHERED TO Y/N
IF NOT WHY NOT?

_____
_____

_____

LESSONS I LEARNED FROM THIS TRADE

_____

_____

_____

_____

_____

_____

WIN/LOSS _____

PROFIT % ON ACCOUNT _____

LOSS % ON ACCOUNT _____

HOW WILL I IMPROVE ON MY NEXT TRADE

_____

_____

_____

VISUAL EXCERCISE (5-10 MINUTES)

PUT ON SOME SOFT MUSIC, LAY BACK AND RELAX AND RECREATE THE TRADE IN YOUR MIND'S EYE.

NOW SEE YOURSELF GOING THROUGH A TRADE BUT NOW YOU ARE IMPLEMENTING THE NEW LESSONS LEARNED FROM THIS TRADE. REPEAT UNTIL YOU AUTOMATICALLY ACT THIS WAY DURING TRADES

TRADER AFFIRMATIONS (SAY 100 TIMES A DAY)

I AM A GREAT TRADER/ I LEARN LESSONS FROM EVERY TRADE AND IMPLEMENT THEM/ I AM A CONSTANTLY IMPROVING TRADER/ I AIM FOR EXCELLENCE IN EVERY TRADE.

DATE _____ TIME _____

DEMO/REAL   INSTRUMENT _____

SETUP
_____
_____
_____

A/B/C GRADE TRADE   RANDOM TRADE?
STOP ADHERED TO Y/N
IF NOT WHY NOT?
_____
_____
_____

TAKE PROFIT ADHERED TO Y/N
IF NOT WHY NOT?
_____
_____
_____

BREAK EVEN ADHERED TO Y/N
IF NOT WHY NOT?
_____
_____
_____

LESSONS I LEARNED FROM THIS TRADE

_____
_____
_____
_____
_____
_____

WIN/LOSS _____

PROFIT % ON ACCOUNT _____

LOSS % ON ACCOUNT _____

HOW WILL I IMPROVE ON MY NEXT TRADE

_____
_____
_____

VISUAL EXCERCISE (5-10 MINUTES)

PUT ON SOME SOFT MUSIC, LAY BACK AND RELAX AND RECREATE THE TRADE IN YOUR MIND'S EYE.

NOW SEE YOURSELF GOING THROUGH A TRADE BUT NOW YOU ARE IMPLEMENTING THE NEW LESSONS LEARNED FROM THIS TRADE. REPEAT UNTIL YOU AUTOMATICALLY ACT THIS WAY DURING TRADES

TRADER AFFIRMATIONS (SAY 100 TIMES A DAY)

I AM A GREAT TRADER/ I LEARN LESSONS FROM EVERY TRADE AND IMPLEMENT THEM/ I AM A CONSTANTLY IMPROVING TRADER/ I AIM FOR EXCELLENCE IN EVERY TRADE.

DATE _____ TIME _____

DEMO/REAL   INSTRUMENT _____

SETUP
_____
_____
_____

A/B/C GRADE TRADE   RANDOM TRADE?

STOP ADHERED TO Y/N

IF NOT WHY NOT?
_____
_____
_____

TAKE PROFIT ADHERED TO Y/N

IF NOT WHY NOT?
_____
_____
_____

BREAK EVEN ADHERED TO Y/N

IF NOT WHY NOT?
_____
_____
_____

LESSONS I LEARNED FROM THIS TRADE

_____
_____
_____
_____
_____

WIN/LOSS _____

PROFIT % ON ACCOUNT _____

LOSS % ON ACCOUNT _____

HOW WILL I IMPROVE ON MY NEXT TRADE

_____
_____
_____

VISUAL EXCERCISE (5-10 MINUTES)

PUT ON SOME SOFT MUSIC, LAY BACK AND RELAX AND RECREATE THE TRADE IN YOUR MIND'S EYE.

NOW SEE YOURSELF GOING THROUGH A TRADE BUT NOW YOU ARE IMPLEMENTING THE NEW LESSONS LEARNED FROM THIS TRADE. REPEAT UNTIL YOU AUTOMATICALLY ACT THIS WAY DURING TRADES

TRADER AFFIRMATIONS (SAY 100 TIMES A DAY)

I AM A GREAT TRADER/ I LEARN LESSONS FROM EVERY TRADE AND IMPLEMENT THEM/ I AM A CONSTANTLY IMPROVING TRADER/ I AIM FOR EXCELLENCE IN EVERY TRADE.

DATE _____ TIME _____

DEMO/REAL   INSTRUMENT _____

SETUP
_____
_____
_____

A/B/C GRADE TRADE   RANDOM TRADE?

STOP ADHERED TO Y/N

IF NOT WHY NOT?
_____
_____
_____

TAKE PROFIT ADHERED TO Y/N

IF NOT WHY NOT?
_____
_____
_____

BREAK EVEN ADHERED TO Y/N

IF NOT WHY NOT?
_____
_____
_____

LESSONS I LEARNED FROM THIS TRADE

_____
_____
_____
_____
_____
_____

WIN/LOSS _____
PROFIT % ON ACCOUNT _____
LOSS % ON ACCOUNT _____

HOW WILL I IMPROVE ON MY NEXT TRADE
_____
_____
_____

VISUAL EXCERCISE (5-10 MINUTES)

PUT ON SOME SOFT MUSIC, LAY BACK AND RELAX AND RECREATE THE TRADE IN YOUR MIND'S EYE.

NOW SEE YOURSELF GOING THROUGH A TRADE BUT NOW YOU ARE IMPLEMENTING THE NEW LESSONS LEARNED FROM THIS TRADE. REPEAT UNTIL YOU AUTOMATICALLY ACT THIS WAY DURING TRADES

TRADER AFFIRMATIONS (SAY 100 TIMES A DAY)

I AM A GREAT TRADER/ I LEARN LESSONS FROM EVERY TRADE AND IMPLEMENT THEM/ I AM A CONSTANTLY IMPROVING TRADER/ I AIM FOR EXCELLENCE IN EVERY TRADE.

DATE _____ TIME _____

DEMO/REAL   INSTRUMENT _____

SETUP
_____
_____
_____

A/B/C GRADE TRADE   RANDOM TRADE?

STOP ADHERED TO Y/N

IF NOT WHY NOT?
_____
_____
_____

TAKE PROFIT ADHERED TO Y/N

IF NOT WHY NOT?
_____
_____
_____

BREAK EVEN ADHERED TO Y/N

IF NOT WHY NOT?
_____
_____
_____

LESSONS I LEARNED FROM THIS TRADE
_____
_____
_____
_____
_____
_____

WIN/LOSS _____
PROFIT % ON ACCOUNT _____
LOSS % ON ACCOUNT _____

HOW WILL I IMPROVE ON MY NEXT TRADE
_____
_____
_____

VISUAL EXCERCISE (5-10 MINUTES)

PUT ON SOME SOFT MUSIC, LAY BACK AND RELAX AND RECREATE THE TRADE IN YOUR MIND'S EYE.

NOW SEE YOURSELF GOING THROUGH A TRADE BUT NOW YOU ARE IMPLEMENTING THE NEW LESSONS LEARNED FROM THIS TRADE. REPEAT UNTIL YOU AUTOMATICALLY ACT THIS WAY DURING TRADES

TRADER AFFIRMATIONS (SAY 100 TIMES A DAY)

I AM A GREAT TRADER/ I LEARN LESSONS FROM EVERY TRADE AND IMPLEMENT THEM/ I AM A CONSTANTLY IMPROVING TRADER/ I AIM FOR EXCELLENCE IN EVERY TRADE.

DATE _____ TIME _____

DEMO/REAL   INSTRUMENT _____

SETUP
_____
_____
_____

A/B/C GRADE TRADE   RANDOM TRADE?
  STOP ADHERED TO Y/N
  IF NOT WHY NOT?
_____
_____
_____

TAKE PROFIT ADHERED TO Y/N
IF NOT WHY NOT?
_____
_____
_____

BREAK EVEN ADHERED TO Y/N
IF NOT WHY NOT?
_____
_____
_____

LESSONS I LEARNED FROM THIS TRADE

_____
_____
_____
_____
_____
_____

WIN/LOSS _____
PROFIT % ON ACCOUNT _____
LOSS % ON ACCOUNT _____

HOW WILL I IMPROVE ON MY NEXT TRADE

_____
_____
_____

VISUAL EXCERCISE (5-10 MINUTES)

PUT ON SOME SOFT MUSIC, LAY BACK AND RELAX AND RECREATE THE TRADE IN YOUR MIND'S EYE.
NOW SEE YOURSELF GOING THROUGH A TRADE BUT NOW YOU ARE IMPLEMENTING THE NEW LESSONS LEARNED FROM THIS TRADE. REPEAT UNTIL YOU AUTOMATICALLY ACT THIS WAY DURING TRADES

TRADER AFFIRMATIONS (SAY 100 TIMES A DAY)

I AM A GREAT TRADER/ I LEARN LESSONS FROM EVERY TRADE AND IMPLEMENT THEM/ I AM A CONSTANTLY IMPROVING TRADER/ I AIM FOR EXCELLENCE IN EVERY TRADE.

DATE _____   TIME _____

DEMO/REAL   INSTRUMENT _____

SETUP
_____
_____
_____

A/B/C GRADE TRADE   RANDOM TRADE?
   STOP ADHERED TO Y/N
   IF NOT WHY NOT?
_____
_____
_____

TAKE PROFIT ADHERED TO Y/N
IF NOT WHY NOT?
_____
_____
_____

BREAK EVEN ADHERED TO Y/N
IF NOT WHY NOT?
_____
_____
_____

LESSONS I LEARNED FROM THIS TRADE

_____
_____
_____
_____
_____
_____

WIN/LOSS _____
PROFIT % ON ACCOUNT _____
LOSS % ON ACCOUNT _____

HOW WILL I IMPROVE ON MY NEXT TRADE

_____
_____
_____

VISUAL EXCERCISE (5-10 MINUTES)

PUT ON SOME SOFT MUSIC, LAY BACK AND RELAX AND RECREATE THE TRADE IN YOUR MIND'S EYE.

NOW SEE YOURSELF GOING THROUGH A TRADE BUT NOW YOU ARE IMPLEMENTING THE NEW LESSONS LEARNED FROM THIS TRADE. REPEAT UNTIL YOU AUTOMATICALLY ACT THIS WAY DURING TRADES

TRADER AFFIRMATIONS (SAY 100 TIMES A DAY)

I AM A GREAT TRADER/ I LEARN LESSONS FROM EVERY TRADE AND IMPLEMENT THEM/ I AM A CONSTANTLY IMPROVING TRADER/ I AIM FOR EXCELLENCE IN EVERY TRADE.

DATE _____ TIME _____

DEMO/REAL   INSTRUMENT _____

SETUP
_____
_____

A/B/C GRADE TRADE   RANDOM TRADE?

STOP ADHERED TO Y/N

IF NOT WHY NOT?
_____
_____

TAKE PROFIT ADHERED TO Y/N

IF NOT WHY NOT?
_____
_____
_____

BREAK EVEN ADHERED TO Y/N

IF NOT WHY NOT?
_____
_____
_____

LESSONS I LEARNED FROM THIS TRADE

_____
_____
_____
_____
_____
_____

WIN/LOSS _____

PROFIT % ON ACCOUNT _____

LOSS % ON ACCOUNT _____

HOW WILL I IMPROVE ON MY NEXT TRADE

_____
_____
_____

VISUAL EXCERCISE (5-10 MINUTES)

PUT ON SOME SOFT MUSIC, LAY BACK AND RELAX AND RECREATE THE TRADE IN YOUR MIND'S EYE.

NOW SEE YOURSELF GOING THROUGH A TRADE BUT NOW YOU ARE IMPLEMENTING THE NEW LESSONS LEARNED FROM THIS TRADE. REPEAT UNTIL YOU AUTOMATICALLY ACT THIS WAY DURING TRADES

TRADER AFFIRMATIONS (SAY 100 TIMES A DAY)

I AM A GREAT TRADER/ I LEARN LESSONS FROM EVERY TRADE AND IMPLEMENT THEM/ I AM A CONSTANTLY IMPROVING TRADER/ I AIM FOR EXCELLENCE IN EVERY TRADE.

DATE _____ TIME _____

DEMO/REAL   INSTRUMENT _____

SETUP
_____
_____
_____

A/B/C GRADE TRADE   RANDOM TRADE?

STOP ADHERED TO Y/N

IF NOT WHY NOT?
_____
_____
_____

TAKE PROFIT ADHERED TO Y/N

IF NOT WHY NOT?
_____
_____
_____

BREAK EVEN ADHERED TO Y/N

IF NOT WHY NOT?
_____
_____
_____

LESSONS I LEARNED FROM THIS TRADE

_____

_____

_____

_____

_____

_____

WIN/LOSS _____

PROFIT % ON ACCOUNT _____

LOSS % ON ACCOUNT _____

HOW WILL I IMPROVE ON MY NEXT TRADE

_____

_____

_____

VISUAL EXCERCISE (5-10 MINUTES)

PUT ON SOME SOFT MUSIC, LAY BACK AND RELAX AND RECREATE THE TRADE IN YOUR MIND'S EYE.
NOW SEE YOURSELF GOING THROUGH A TRADE BUT NOW YOU ARE IMPLEMENTING THE NEW LESSONS LEARNED FROM THIS TRADE. REPEAT UNTIL YOU AUTOMATICALLY ACT THIS WAY DURING TRADES

TRADER AFFIRMATIONS (SAY 100 TIMES A DAY)

I AM A GREAT TRADER/ I LEARN LESSONS FROM EVERY TRADE AND IMPLEMENT THEM/ I AM A CONSTANTLY IMPROVING TRADER/ I AIM FOR EXCELLENCE IN EVERY TRADE.

DATE _____ TIME _____

DEMO/REAL   INSTRUMENT _____

SETUP
_____
_____
_____

A/B/C GRADE TRADE   RANDOM TRADE?
STOP ADHERED TO Y/N
IF NOT WHY NOT?
_____
_____
_____

TAKE PROFIT ADHERED TO Y/N
IF NOT WHY NOT?
_____
_____
_____

BREAK EVEN ADHERED TO Y/N
IF NOT WHY NOT?
_____
_____
_____

LESSONS I LEARNED FROM THIS TRADE

_____

_____

_____

_____

_____

_____

WIN/LOSS _____

PROFIT % ON ACCOUNT _____

LOSS % ON ACCOUNT _____

HOW WILL I IMPROVE ON MY NEXT TRADE

_____

_____

_____

VISUAL EXCERCISE (5-10 MINUTES)

PUT ON SOME SOFT MUSIC, LAY BACK AND RELAX AND RECREATE THE TRADE IN YOUR MIND'S EYE.

NOW SEE YOURSELF GOING THROUGH A TRADE BUT NOW YOU ARE IMPLEMENTING THE NEW LESSONS LEARNED FROM THIS TRADE. REPEAT UNTIL YOU AUTOMATICALLY ACT THIS WAY DURING TRADES

TRADER AFFIRMATIONS (SAY 100 TIMES A DAY)

I AM A GREAT TRADER/ I LEARN LESSONS FROM EVERY TRADE AND IMPLEMENT THEM/ I AM A CONSTANTLY IMPROVING TRADER/ I AIM FOR EXCELLENCE IN EVERY TRADE.

DATE _____   TIME _____

DEMO/REAL   INSTRUMENT _____

SETUP
_____
_____
_____

A/B/C GRADE TRADE   RANDOM TRADE?

STOP ADHERED TO Y/N

IF NOT WHY NOT?
_____
_____
_____

TAKE PROFIT ADHERED TO Y/N

IF NOT WHY NOT?
_____
_____
_____

BREAK EVEN ADHERED TO Y/N

IF NOT WHY NOT?
_____
_____
_____

LESSONS I LEARNED FROM THIS TRADE

_____

_____

_____

_____

_____

_____

WIN/LOSS _____

PROFIT % ON ACCOUNT _____

LOSS % ON ACCOUNT _____

HOW WILL I IMPROVE ON MY NEXT TRADE

_____

_____

_____

VISUAL EXCERCISE (5-10 MINUTES)

PUT ON SOME SOFT MUSIC, LAY BACK AND RELAX AND RECREATE THE TRADE IN YOUR MIND'S EYE.

NOW SEE YOURSELF GOING THROUGH A TRADE BUT NOW YOU ARE IMPLEMENTING THE NEW LESSONS LEARNED FROM THIS TRADE. REPEAT UNTIL YOU AUTOMATICALLY ACT THIS WAY DURING TRADES

TRADER AFFIRMATIONS (SAY 100 TIMES A DAY)

I AM A GREAT TRADER/ I LEARN LESSONS FROM EVERY TRADE AND IMPLEMENT THEM/ I AM A CONSTANTLY IMPROVING TRADER/ I AIM FOR EXCELLENCE IN EVERY TRADE.

DATE _____   TIME _____

DEMO/REAL   INSTRUMENT _____

SETUP
_____
_____
_____

A/B/C GRADE TRADE   RANDOM TRADE?
STOP ADHERED TO Y/N
IF NOT WHY NOT?
_____
_____
_____

TAKE PROFIT ADHERED TO Y/N
IF NOT WHY NOT?
_____
_____
_____

BREAK EVEN ADHERED TO Y/N
IF NOT WHY NOT?
_____
_____
_____

LESSONS I LEARNED FROM THIS TRADE

_____
_____
_____
_____
_____
_____

WIN/LOSS _____
PROFIT % ON ACCOUNT _____
LOSS % ON ACCOUNT _____

HOW WILL I IMPROVE ON MY NEXT TRADE
_____
_____
_____

VISUAL EXCERCISE (5-10 MINUTES)

PUT ON SOME SOFT MUSIC, LAY BACK AND RELAX AND RECREATE THE TRADE IN YOUR MIND'S EYE.
NOW SEE YOURSELF GOING THROUGH A TRADE BUT NOW YOU ARE IMPLEMENTING THE NEW LESSONS LEARNED FROM THIS TRADE. REPEAT UNTIL YOU AUTOMATICALLY ACT THIS WAY DURING TRADES

TRADER AFFIRMATIONS (SAY 100 TIMES A DAY)

I AM A GREAT TRADER/ I LEARN LESSONS FROM EVERY TRADE AND IMPLEMENT THEM/ I AM A CONSTANTLY IMPROVING TRADER/ I AIM FOR EXCELLENCE IN EVERY TRADE.

DATE _____ TIME _____

DEMO/REAL   INSTRUMENT _____

SETUP
_____
_____
_____

A/B/C GRADE TRADE   RANDOM TRADE?

STOP ADHERED TO Y/N

IF NOT WHY NOT?
_____
_____
_____

TAKE PROFIT ADHERED TO Y/N

IF NOT WHY NOT?
_____
_____
_____

BREAK EVEN ADHERED TO Y/N

IF NOT WHY NOT?
_____
_____
_____

LESSONS I LEARNED FROM THIS TRADE

_____
_____
_____
_____
_____

WIN/LOSS _____
PROFIT % ON ACCOUNT _____
LOSS % ON ACCOUNT _____

HOW WILL I IMPROVE ON MY NEXT TRADE
_____
_____
_____

VISUAL EXCERCISE (5-10 MINUTES)

PUT ON SOME SOFT MUSIC, LAY BACK AND RELAX AND RECREATE THE TRADE IN YOUR MIND'S EYE.
NOW SEE YOURSELF GOING THROUGH A TRADE BUT NOW YOU ARE IMPLEMENTING THE NEW LESSONS LEARNED FROM THIS TRADE. REPEAT UNTIL YOU AUTOMATICALLY ACT THIS WAY DURING TRADES

TRADER AFFIRMATIONS (SAY 100 TIMES A DAY)

I AM A GREAT TRADER/ I LEARN LESSONS FROM EVERY TRADE AND IMPLEMENT THEM/ I AM A CONSTANTLY IMPROVING TRADER/ I AIM FOR EXCELLENCE IN EVERY TRADE.

DATE _____ TIME _____

DEMO/REAL   INSTRUMENT _____

SETUP
_____
_____
_____

A/B/C GRADE TRADE   RANDOM TRADE?

STOP ADHERED TO Y/N

IF NOT WHY NOT?
_____
_____
_____

TAKE PROFIT ADHERED TO Y/N

IF NOT WHY NOT?
_____
_____
_____

BREAK EVEN ADHERED TO Y/N

IF NOT WHY NOT?
_____
_____
_____

LESSONS I LEARNED FROM THIS TRADE

_____
_____
_____
_____
_____
_____

WIN/LOSS _____

PROFIT % ON ACCOUNT _____

LOSS % ON ACCOUNT _____

HOW WILL I IMPROVE ON MY NEXT TRADE

_____
_____
_____

VISUAL EXCERCISE (5-10 MINUTES)

PUT ON SOME SOFT MUSIC, LAY BACK AND RELAX AND RECREATE THE TRADE IN YOUR MIND'S EYE.

NOW SEE YOURSELF GOING THROUGH A TRADE BUT NOW YOU ARE IMPLEMENTING THE NEW LESSONS LEARNED FROM THIS TRADE. REPEAT UNTIL YOU AUTOMATICALLY ACT THIS WAY DURING TRADES

TRADER AFFIRMATIONS (SAY 100 TIMES A DAY)

I AM A GREAT TRADER/ I LEARN LESSONS FROM EVERY TRADE AND IMPLEMENT THEM/ I AM A CONSTANTLY IMPROVING TRADER/ I AIM FOR EXCELLENCE IN EVERY TRADE.

DATE _____ TIME _____

DEMO/REAL   INSTRUMENT _____

SETUP
_____
_____
_____

A/B/C GRADE TRADE   RANDOM TRADE?

STOP ADHERED TO Y/N

IF NOT WHY NOT?
_____
_____
_____

TAKE PROFIT ADHERED TO Y/N

IF NOT WHY NOT?
_____
_____
_____

BREAK EVEN ADHERED TO Y/N

IF NOT WHY NOT?
_____
_____
_____

LESSONS I LEARNED FROM THIS TRADE

_____
_____
_____
_____
_____
_____

WIN/LOSS _____
PROFIT % ON ACCOUNT _____
LOSS % ON ACCOUNT _____

HOW WILL I IMPROVE ON MY NEXT TRADE

_____
_____
_____

VISUAL EXCERCISE (5-10 MINUTES)

PUT ON SOME SOFT MUSIC, LAY BACK AND RELAX AND RECREATE THE TRADE IN YOUR MIND'S EYE.

NOW SEE YOURSELF GOING THROUGH A TRADE BUT NOW YOU ARE IMPLEMENTING THE NEW LESSONS LEARNED FROM THIS TRADE. REPEAT UNTIL YOU AUTOMATICALLY ACT THIS WAY DURING TRADES

TRADER AFFIRMATIONS (SAY 100 TIMES A DAY)

I AM A GREAT TRADER/ I LEARN LESSONS FROM EVERY TRADE AND IMPLEMENT THEM/ I AM A CONSTANTLY IMPROVING TRADER/ I AIM FOR EXCELLENCE IN EVERY TRADE.

DATE _____ TIME _____

DEMO/REAL   INSTRUMENT _____

SETUP
_____
_____
_____

A/B/C GRADE TRADE   RANDOM TRADE?
  STOP ADHERED TO Y/N
  IF NOT WHY NOT?
_____
_____
_____

TAKE PROFIT ADHERED TO Y/N
IF NOT WHY NOT?
_____
_____
_____

BREAK EVEN ADHERED TO Y/N
IF NOT WHY NOT?
_____
_____
_____

LESSONS I LEARNED FROM THIS TRADE

_____
_____
_____
_____
_____
_____

WIN/LOSS _____

PROFIT % ON ACCOUNT _____

LOSS % ON ACCOUNT _____

HOW WILL I IMPROVE ON MY NEXT TRADE

_____
_____
_____

VISUAL EXCERCISE (5-10 MINUTES)

PUT ON SOME SOFT MUSIC, LAY BACK AND RELAX AND RECREATE THE TRADE IN YOUR MIND'S EYE.

NOW SEE YOURSELF GOING THROUGH A TRADE BUT NOW YOU ARE IMPLEMENTING THE NEW LESSONS LEARNED FROM THIS TRADE. REPEAT UNTIL YOU AUTOMATICALLY ACT THIS WAY DURING TRADES

TRADER AFFIRMATIONS (SAY 100 TIMES A DAY)

I AM A GREAT TRADER/ I LEARN LESSONS FROM EVERY TRADE AND IMPLEMENT THEM/ I AM A CONSTANTLY IMPROVING TRADER/ I AIM FOR EXCELLENCE IN EVERY TRADE.

DATE _____   TIME _____

DEMO/REAL   INSTRUMENT _____

SETUP
_____
_____
_____

A/B/C GRADE TRADE   RANDOM TRADE?

STOP ADHERED TO Y/N

IF NOT WHY NOT?
_____
_____
_____

TAKE PROFIT ADHERED TO Y/N

IF NOT WHY NOT?
_____
_____
_____

BREAK EVEN ADHERED TO Y/N

IF NOT WHY NOT?
_____
_____
_____

LESSONS I LEARNED FROM THIS TRADE

_____
_____
_____
_____
_____
_____

WIN/LOSS _____

PROFIT % ON ACCOUNT _____

LOSS % ON ACCOUNT _____

HOW WILL I IMPROVE ON MY NEXT TRADE

_____
_____
_____

VISUAL EXCERCISE (5-10 MINUTES)

PUT ON SOME SOFT MUSIC, LAY BACK AND RELAX AND RECREATE THE TRADE IN YOUR MIND'S EYE.

NOW SEE YOURSELF GOING THROUGH A TRADE BUT NOW YOU ARE IMPLEMENTING THE NEW LESSONS LEARNED FROM THIS TRADE. REPEAT UNTIL YOU AUTOMATICALLY ACT THIS WAY DURING TRADES

TRADER AFFIRMATIONS (SAY 100 TIMES A DAY)

I AM A GREAT TRADER/ I LEARN LESSONS FROM EVERY TRADE AND IMPLEMENT THEM/ I AM A CONSTANTLY IMPROVING TRADER/ I AIM FOR EXCELLENCE IN EVERY TRADE.

DATE _____ TIME _____

DEMO/REAL   INSTRUMENT _____

SETUP
_____
_____

A/B/C GRADE TRADE   RANDOM TRADE?
STOP ADHERED TO Y/N
IF NOT WHY NOT?
_____
_____

TAKE PROFIT ADHERED TO Y/N
IF NOT WHY NOT?
_____
_____

BREAK EVEN ADHERED TO Y/N
IF NOT WHY NOT?
_____
_____
_____

LESSONS I LEARNED FROM THIS TRADE

_____
_____
_____
_____
_____
_____

WIN/LOSS _____
PROFIT % ON ACCOUNT _____
LOSS % ON ACCOUNT _____

HOW WILL I IMPROVE ON MY NEXT TRADE

_____
_____
_____

VISUAL EXCERCISE (5-10 MINUTES)

PUT ON SOME SOFT MUSIC, LAY BACK AND RELAX AND RECREATE THE TRADE IN YOUR MIND'S EYE.
NOW SEE YOURSELF GOING THROUGH A TRADE BUT NOW YOU ARE IMPLEMENTING THE NEW LESSONS LEARNED FROM THIS TRADE. REPEAT UNTIL YOU AUTOMATICALLY ACT THIS WAY DURING TRADES

TRADER AFFIRMATIONS (SAY 100 TIMES A DAY)

I AM A GREAT TRADER/ I LEARN LESSONS FROM EVERY TRADE AND IMPLEMENT THEM/ I AM A CONSTANTLY IMPROVING TRADER/ I AIM FOR EXCELLENCE IN EVERY TRADE.

DATE _____ TIME _____

DEMO/REAL   INSTRUMENT _____

SETUP
_____
_____
_____

A/B/C GRADE TRADE   RANDOM TRADE?

STOP ADHERED TO Y/N

IF NOT WHY NOT?
_____
_____
_____

TAKE PROFIT ADHERED TO Y/N

IF NOT WHY NOT?
_____
_____
_____

BREAK EVEN ADHERED TO Y/N

IF NOT WHY NOT?
_____
_____
_____

LESSONS I LEARNED FROM THIS TRADE

_____

_____

_____

_____

_____

_____

WIN/LOSS _____

PROFIT % ON ACCOUNT _____

LOSS % ON ACCOUNT _____

HOW WILL I IMPROVE ON MY NEXT TRADE

_____

_____

_____

VISUAL EXCERCISE (5-10 MINUTES)

PUT ON SOME SOFT MUSIC, LAY BACK AND RELAX AND RECREATE THE TRADE IN YOUR MIND'S EYE.

NOW SEE YOURSELF GOING THROUGH A TRADE BUT NOW YOU ARE IMPLEMENTING THE NEW LESSONS LEARNED FROM THIS TRADE. REPEAT UNTIL YOU AUTOMATICALLY ACT THIS WAY DURING TRADES

TRADER AFFIRMATIONS (SAY 100 TIMES A DAY)

I AM A GREAT TRADER/ I LEARN LESSONS FROM EVERY TRADE AND IMPLEMENT THEM/ I AM A CONSTANTLY IMPROVING TRADER/ I AIM FOR EXCELLENCE IN EVERY TRADE.

DATE _____ TIME _____

DEMO/REAL   INSTRUMENT _____

SETUP
_____
_____
_____

A/B/C GRADE TRADE   RANDOM TRADE?
STOP ADHERED TO Y/N
IF NOT WHY NOT?
_____
_____
_____

TAKE PROFIT ADHERED TO Y/N
IF NOT WHY NOT?
_____
_____
_____

BREAK EVEN ADHERED TO Y/N
IF NOT WHY NOT?
_____
_____
_____

LESSONS I LEARNED FROM THIS TRADE

_____
_____
_____
_____
_____
_____

WIN/LOSS _____

PROFIT % ON ACCOUNT _____

LOSS % ON ACCOUNT _____

HOW WILL I IMPROVE ON MY NEXT TRADE

_____
_____
_____

VISUAL EXCERCISE (5-10 MINUTES)

PUT ON SOME SOFT MUSIC, LAY BACK AND RELAX AND RECREATE THE TRADE IN YOUR MIND'S EYE.

NOW SEE YOURSELF GOING THROUGH A TRADE BUT NOW YOU ARE IMPLEMENTING THE NEW LESSONS LEARNED FROM THIS TRADE. REPEAT UNTIL YOU AUTOMATICALLY ACT THIS WAY DURING TRADES

TRADER AFFIRMATIONS (SAY 100 TIMES A DAY)

I AM A GREAT TRADER/ I LEARN LESSONS FROM EVERY TRADE AND IMPLEMENT THEM/ I AM A CONSTANTLY IMPROVING TRADER/ I AIM FOR EXCELLENCE IN EVERY TRADE.

DATE _____ TIME _____

DEMO/REAL   INSTRUMENT _____

SETUP
_____
_____
_____

A/B/C GRADE TRADE   RANDOM TRADE?

STOP ADHERED TO Y/N

IF NOT WHY NOT?
_____
_____
_____

TAKE PROFIT ADHERED TO Y/N

IF NOT WHY NOT?
_____
_____
_____

BREAK EVEN ADHERED TO Y/N

IF NOT WHY NOT?
_____
_____
_____

LESSONS I LEARNED FROM THIS TRADE

_____
_____
_____
_____
_____

WIN/LOSS _____
PROFIT % ON ACCOUNT _____
LOSS % ON ACCOUNT _____

HOW WILL I IMPROVE ON MY NEXT TRADE
_____
_____
_____

VISUAL EXCERCISE (5-10 MINUTES)

PUT ON SOME SOFT MUSIC, LAY BACK AND RELAX AND RECREATE THE TRADE IN YOUR MIND'S EYE.
NOW SEE YOURSELF GOING THROUGH A TRADE BUT NOW YOU ARE IMPLEMENTING THE NEW LESSONS LEARNED FROM THIS TRADE. REPEAT UNTIL YOU AUTOMATICALLY ACT THIS WAY DURING TRADES

TRADER AFFIRMATIONS (SAY 100 TIMES A DAY)

I AM A GREAT TRADER/ I LEARN LESSONS FROM EVERY TRADE AND IMPLEMENT THEM/ I AM A CONSTANTLY IMPROVING TRADER/ I AIM FOR EXCELLENCE IN EVERY TRADE.

DATE _____ TIME _____

DEMO/REAL   INSTRUMENT _____

SETUP
_____
_____
_____

A/B/C GRADE TRADE   RANDOM TRADE?

STOP ADHERED TO Y/N

IF NOT WHY NOT?
_____
_____
_____

TAKE PROFIT ADHERED TO Y/N

IF NOT WHY NOT?
_____
_____
_____

BREAK EVEN ADHERED TO Y/N

IF NOT WHY NOT?
_____
_____
_____

LESSONS I LEARNED FROM THIS TRADE

_____
_____
_____
_____
_____
_____

WIN/LOSS _____
PROFIT % ON ACCOUNT _____
LOSS % ON ACCOUNT _____

HOW WILL I IMPROVE ON MY NEXT TRADE
_____
_____
_____

VISUAL EXCERCISE (5-10 MINUTES)

PUT ON SOME SOFT MUSIC, LAY BACK AND RELAX AND RECREATE THE TRADE IN YOUR MIND'S EYE.

NOW SEE YOURSELF GOING THROUGH A TRADE BUT NOW YOU ARE IMPLEMENTING THE NEW LESSONS LEARNED FROM THIS TRADE. REPEAT UNTIL YOU AUTOMATICALLY ACT THIS WAY DURING TRADES

TRADER AFFIRMATIONS (SAY 100 TIMES A DAY)

I AM A GREAT TRADER/ I LEARN LESSONS FROM EVERY TRADE AND IMPLEMENT THEM/ I AM A CONSTANTLY IMPROVING TRADER/ I AIM FOR EXCELLENCE IN EVERY TRADE.

DATE _____ TIME _____

DEMO/REAL   INSTRUMENT _____

SETUP
_____
_____

_____

A/B/C GRADE TRADE   RANDOM TRADE?
STOP ADHERED TO Y/N
IF NOT WHY NOT?
_____
_____

_____

TAKE PROFIT ADHERED TO Y/N
IF NOT WHY NOT?
_____
_____

_____

BREAK EVEN ADHERED TO Y/N
IF NOT WHY NOT?
_____
_____

_____

LESSONS I LEARNED FROM THIS TRADE

_____
_____
_____
_____
_____
_____

WIN/LOSS _____
PROFIT % ON ACCOUNT _____
LOSS % ON ACCOUNT _____

HOW WILL I IMPROVE ON MY NEXT TRADE
_____
_____
_____

VISUAL EXCERCISE (5-10 MINUTES)

PUT ON SOME SOFT MUSIC, LAY BACK AND RELAX AND RECREATE THE TRADE IN YOUR MIND'S EYE.

NOW SEE YOURSELF GOING THROUGH A TRADE BUT NOW YOU ARE IMPLEMENTING THE NEW LESSONS LEARNED FROM THIS TRADE. REPEAT UNTIL YOU AUTOMATICALLY ACT THIS WAY DURING TRADES

TRADER AFFIRMATIONS (SAY 100 TIMES A DAY)

I AM A GREAT TRADER/ I LEARN LESSONS FROM EVERY TRADE AND IMPLEMENT THEM/ I AM A CONSTANTLY IMPROVING TRADER/ I AIM FOR EXCELLENCE IN EVERY TRADE.

DATE _____ TIME _____

DEMO/REAL   INSTRUMENT _____

SETUP
_____
_____
_____

A/B/C GRADE TRADE   RANDOM TRADE?

STOP ADHERED TO Y/N

IF NOT WHY NOT?
_____
_____
_____

TAKE PROFIT ADHERED TO Y/N

IF NOT WHY NOT?
_____
_____
_____

BREAK EVEN ADHERED TO Y/N

IF NOT WHY NOT?
_____
_____
_____

LESSONS I LEARNED FROM THIS TRADE

_____
_____
_____
_____
_____
_____

WIN/LOSS _____
PROFIT % ON ACCOUNT _____
LOSS % ON ACCOUNT _____

HOW WILL I IMPROVE ON MY NEXT TRADE

_____
_____
_____

VISUAL EXCERCISE (5-10 MINUTES)

PUT ON SOME SOFT MUSIC, LAY BACK AND RELAX AND RECREATE THE TRADE IN YOUR MIND'S EYE.

NOW SEE YOURSELF GOING THROUGH A TRADE BUT NOW YOU ARE IMPLEMENTING THE NEW LESSONS LEARNED FROM THIS TRADE. REPEAT UNTIL YOU AUTOMATICALLY ACT THIS WAY DURING TRADES

TRADER AFFIRMATIONS (SAY 100 TIMES A DAY)

I AM A GREAT TRADER/ I LEARN LESSONS FROM EVERY TRADE AND IMPLEMENT THEM/ I AM A CONSTANTLY IMPROVING TRADER/ I AIM FOR EXCELLENCE IN EVERY TRADE.

DATE _____ TIME _____

DEMO/REAL   INSTRUMENT _____

SETUP
_____
_____
_____

A/B/C GRADE TRADE   RANDOM TRADE?

STOP ADHERED TO Y/N

IF NOT WHY NOT?
_____
_____
_____

TAKE PROFIT ADHERED TO Y/N

IF NOT WHY NOT?
_____
_____
_____

BREAK EVEN ADHERED TO Y/N

IF NOT WHY NOT?
_____
_____
_____

LESSONS I LEARNED FROM THIS TRADE

_____
_____
_____
_____
_____
_____

WIN/LOSS
PROFIT % ON ACCOUNT
LOSS % ON ACCOUNT

HOW WILL I IMPROVE ON MY NEXT TRADE
_____
_____
_____

VISUAL EXCERCISE (5-10 MINUTES)

PUT ON SOME SOFT MUSIC, LAY BACK AND RELAX AND RECREATE THE TRADE IN YOUR MIND'S EYE.
NOW SEE YOURSELF GOING THROUGH A TRADE BUT NOW YOU ARE IMPLEMENTING THE NEW LESSONS LEARNED FROM THIS TRADE. REPEAT UNTIL YOU AUTOMATICALLY ACT THIS WAY DURING TRADES

TRADER AFFIRMATIONS (SAY 100 TIMES A DAY)

I AM A GREAT TRADER/ I LEARN LESSONS FROM EVERY TRADE AND IMPLEMENT THEM/ I AM A CONSTANTLY IMPROVING TRADER/ I AIM FOR EXCELLENCE IN EVERY TRADE.

DATE _____ TIME _____

DEMO/REAL   INSTRUMENT _____

SETUP
_____
_____
_____

A/B/C GRADE TRADE   RANDOM TRADE?

STOP ADHERED TO Y/N

IF NOT WHY NOT?
_____
_____
_____

TAKE PROFIT ADHERED TO Y/N

IF NOT WHY NOT?
_____
_____
_____

BREAK EVEN ADHERED TO Y/N

IF NOT WHY NOT?
_____
_____
_____

LESSONS I LEARNED FROM THIS TRADE

_____
_____
_____
_____
_____
_____

WIN/LOSS _____
PROFIT % ON ACCOUNT _____
LOSS % ON ACCOUNT _____

HOW WILL I IMPROVE ON MY NEXT TRADE

_____
_____
_____

VISUAL EXCERCISE (5-10 MINUTES)

PUT ON SOME SOFT MUSIC, LAY BACK AND RELAX AND RECREATE THE TRADE IN YOUR MIND'S EYE.
NOW SEE YOURSELF GOING THROUGH A TRADE BUT NOW YOU ARE IMPLEMENTING THE NEW LESSONS LEARNED FROM THIS TRADE. REPEAT UNTIL YOU AUTOMATICALLY ACT THIS WAY DURING TRADES

TRADER AFFIRMATIONS (SAY 100 TIMES A DAY)

I AM A GREAT TRADER/ I LEARN LESSONS FROM EVERY TRADE AND IMPLEMENT THEM/ I AM A CONSTANTLY IMPROVING TRADER/ I AIM FOR EXCELLENCE IN EVERY TRADE.

DATE _____ TIME _____

DEMO/REAL   INSTRUMENT _____

SETUP
_____
_____
_____

A/B/C GRADE TRADE   RANDOM TRADE?
STOP ADHERED TO Y/N
IF NOT WHY NOT?
_____
_____
_____

TAKE PROFIT ADHERED TO Y/N
IF NOT WHY NOT?
_____
_____
_____

BREAK EVEN ADHERED TO Y/N
IF NOT WHY NOT?
_____
_____
_____

LESSONS I LEARNED FROM THIS TRADE

_____
_____
_____
_____
_____
_____

WIN/LOSS _____
PROFIT % ON ACCOUNT _____
LOSS % ON ACCOUNT _____

HOW WILL I IMPROVE ON MY NEXT TRADE
_____
_____
_____

VISUAL EXCERCISE (5-10 MINUTES)

PUT ON SOME SOFT MUSIC, LAY BACK AND RELAX AND RECREATE THE TRADE IN YOUR MIND'S EYE.
NOW SEE YOURSELF GOING THROUGH A TRADE BUT NOW YOU ARE IMPLEMENTING THE NEW LESSONS LEARNED FROM THIS TRADE. REPEAT UNTIL YOU AUTOMATICALLY ACT THIS WAY DURING TRADES

TRADER AFFIRMATIONS (SAY 100 TIMES A DAY)

I AM A GREAT TRADER/ I LEARN LESSONS FROM EVERY TRADE AND IMPLEMENT THEM/ I AM A CONSTANTLY IMPROVING TRADER/ I AIM FOR EXCELLENCE IN EVERY TRADE.

DATE _____ TIME _____

DEMO/REAL   INSTRUMENT _____

SETUP
_____
_____
_____

A/B/C GRADE TRADE   RANDOM TRADE?

STOP ADHERED TO Y/N

IF NOT WHY NOT?
_____
_____
_____

TAKE PROFIT ADHERED TO Y/N

IF NOT WHY NOT?
_____
_____
_____

BREAK EVEN ADHERED TO Y/N

IF NOT WHY NOT?
_____
_____
_____

LESSONS I LEARNED FROM THIS TRADE

_____
_____
_____
_____
_____
_____

WIN/LOSS _____

PROFIT % ON ACCOUNT _____

LOSS % ON ACCOUNT _____

HOW WILL I IMPROVE ON MY NEXT TRADE

_____
_____
_____

VISUAL EXCERCISE (5-10 MINUTES)

PUT ON SOME SOFT MUSIC, LAY BACK AND RELAX AND RECREATE THE TRADE IN YOUR MIND'S EYE.

NOW SEE YOURSELF GOING THROUGH A TRADE BUT NOW YOU ARE IMPLEMENTING THE NEW LESSONS LEARNED FROM THIS TRADE. REPEAT UNTIL YOU AUTOMATICALLY ACT THIS WAY DURING TRADES

TRADER AFFIRMATIONS (SAY 100 TIMES A DAY)

I AM A GREAT TRADER/ I LEARN LESSONS FROM EVERY TRADE AND IMPLEMENT THEM/ I AM A CONSTANTLY IMPROVING TRADER/ I AIM FOR EXCELLENCE IN EVERY TRADE.

DATE _____ TIME _____

DEMO/REAL   INSTRUMENT _____

SETUP
_____
_____
_____

A/B/C GRADE TRADE   RANDOM TRADE?
STOP ADHERED TO Y/N
IF NOT WHY NOT?
_____
_____
_____

TAKE PROFIT ADHERED TO Y/N
IF NOT WHY NOT?
_____
_____
_____

BREAK EVEN ADHERED TO Y/N
IF NOT WHY NOT?
_____
_____
_____

LESSONS I LEARNED FROM THIS TRADE

_____

_____

_____

_____

_____

_____

WIN/LOSS _____

PROFIT % ON ACCOUNT _____

LOSS % ON ACCOUNT _____

HOW WILL I IMPROVE ON MY NEXT TRADE

_____

_____

_____

VISUAL EXCERCISE (5-10 MINUTES)

PUT ON SOME SOFT MUSIC, LAY BACK AND RELAX AND RECREATE THE TRADE IN YOUR MIND'S EYE.

NOW SEE YOURSELF GOING THROUGH A TRADE BUT NOW YOU ARE IMPLEMENTING THE NEW LESSONS LEARNED FROM THIS TRADE. REPEAT UNTIL YOU AUTOMATICALLY ACT THIS WAY DURING TRADES

TRADER AFFIRMATIONS (SAY 100 TIMES A DAY)

I AM A GREAT TRADER/ I LEARN LESSONS FROM EVERY TRADE AND IMPLEMENT THEM/ I AM A CONSTANTLY IMPROVING TRADER/ I AIM FOR EXCELLENCE IN EVERY TRADE.

DATE _____ TIME _____

DEMO/REAL   INSTRUMENT _____

SETUP
_____
_____
_____

A/B/C GRADE TRADE   RANDOM TRADE?

STOP ADHERED TO Y/N

IF NOT WHY NOT?
_____
_____
_____

TAKE PROFIT ADHERED TO Y/N

IF NOT WHY NOT?
_____
_____
_____

BREAK EVEN ADHERED TO Y/N

IF NOT WHY NOT?
_____
_____
_____

LESSONS I LEARNED FROM THIS TRADE

_____
_____
_____
_____
_____
_____

WIN/LOSS _____
PROFIT % ON ACCOUNT _____
LOSS % ON ACCOUNT _____

HOW WILL I IMPROVE ON MY NEXT TRADE
_____
_____
_____

VISUAL EXCERCISE (5-10 MINUTES)

PUT ON SOME SOFT MUSIC, LAY BACK AND RELAX AND RECREATE THE TRADE IN YOUR MIND'S EYE.

NOW SEE YOURSELF GOING THROUGH A TRADE BUT NOW YOU ARE IMPLEMENTING THE NEW LESSONS LEARNED FROM THIS TRADE. REPEAT UNTIL YOU AUTOMATICALLY ACT THIS WAY DURING TRADES

TRADER AFFIRMATIONS (SAY 100 TIMES A DAY)

I AM A GREAT TRADER/ I LEARN LESSONS FROM EVERY TRADE AND IMPLEMENT THEM/ I AM A CONSTANTLY IMPROVING TRADER/ I AIM FOR EXCELLENCE IN EVERY TRADE.

DATE _____ TIME _____

DEMO/REAL INSTRUMENT _____

SETUP

_____

_____

_____

A/B/C GRADE TRADE   RANDOM TRADE?

STOP ADHERED TO Y/N

IF NOT WHY NOT?

_____

_____

_____

TAKE PROFIT ADHERED TO Y/N

IF NOT WHY NOT?

_____

_____

_____

BREAK EVEN ADHERED TO Y/N

IF NOT WHY NOT?

_____

_____

_____

LESSONS I LEARNED FROM THIS TRADE

_____
_____
_____
_____
_____
_____

WIN/LOSS _____
PROFIT % ON ACCOUNT _____
LOSS % ON ACCOUNT _____

HOW WILL I IMPROVE ON MY NEXT TRADE
_____
_____
_____

VISUAL EXCERCISE (5-10 MINUTES)

PUT ON SOME SOFT MUSIC, LAY BACK AND RELAX AND RECREATE THE TRADE IN YOUR MIND'S EYE.
NOW SEE YOURSELF GOING THROUGH A TRADE BUT NOW YOU ARE IMPLEMENTING THE NEW LESSONS LEARNED FROM THIS TRADE. REPEAT UNTIL YOU AUTOMATICALLY ACT THIS WAY DURING TRADES

TRADER AFFIRMATIONS (SAY 100 TIMES A DAY)

I AM A GREAT TRADER/ I LEARN LESSONS FROM EVERY TRADE AND IMPLEMENT THEM/ I AM A CONSTANTLY IMPROVING TRADER/ I AIM FOR EXCELLENCE IN EVERY TRADE.

DATE _____ TIME _____

DEMO/REAL   INSTRUMENT _____

SETUP
_____
_____
_____

A/B/C GRADE TRADE   RANDOM TRADE?
STOP ADHERED TO Y/N
IF NOT WHY NOT?
_____
_____
_____

TAKE PROFIT ADHERED TO Y/N
IF NOT WHY NOT?
_____
_____
_____

BREAK EVEN ADHERED TO Y/N
IF NOT WHY NOT?
_____
_____
_____

LESSONS I LEARNED FROM THIS TRADE

_____
_____
_____
_____
_____
_____

WIN/LOSS _____

PROFIT % ON ACCOUNT _____

LOSS % ON ACCOUNT _____

HOW WILL I IMPROVE ON MY NEXT TRADE

_____
_____
_____

VISUAL EXCERCISE (5-10 MINUTES)

PUT ON SOME SOFT MUSIC, LAY BACK AND RELAX AND RECREATE THE TRADE IN YOUR MIND'S EYE.

NOW SEE YOURSELF GOING THROUGH A TRADE BUT NOW YOU ARE IMPLEMENTING THE NEW LESSONS LEARNED FROM THIS TRADE. REPEAT UNTIL YOU AUTOMATICALLY ACT THIS WAY DURING TRADES

TRADER AFFIRMATIONS (SAY 100 TIMES A DAY)

I AM A GREAT TRADER/ I LEARN LESSONS FROM EVERY TRADE AND IMPLEMENT THEM/ I AM A CONSTANTLY IMPROVING TRADER/ I AIM FOR EXCELLENCE IN EVERY TRADE.

DATE _____ TIME _____

DEMO/REAL   INSTRUMENT _____

SETUP
_____
_____
_____

A/B/C GRADE TRADE   RANDOM TRADE?

STOP ADHERED TO Y/N

IF NOT WHY NOT?
_____
_____
_____

TAKE PROFIT ADHERED TO Y/N

IF NOT WHY NOT?
_____
_____
_____

BREAK EVEN ADHERED TO Y/N

IF NOT WHY NOT?
_____
_____
_____

LESSONS I LEARNED FROM THIS TRADE

_____
_____
_____
_____
_____
_____

WIN/LOSS _____
PROFIT % ON ACCOUNT _____
LOSS % ON ACCOUNT _____

HOW WILL I IMPROVE ON MY NEXT TRADE
_____
_____
_____

VISUAL EXCERCISE (5-10 MINUTES)

PUT ON SOME SOFT MUSIC, LAY BACK AND RELAX AND RECREATE THE TRADE IN YOUR MIND'S EYE.

NOW SEE YOURSELF GOING THROUGH A TRADE BUT NOW YOU ARE IMPLEMENTING THE NEW LESSONS LEARNED FROM THIS TRADE. REPEAT UNTIL YOU AUTOMATICALLY ACT THIS WAY DURING TRADES

TRADER AFFIRMATIONS (SAY 100 TIMES A DAY)

I AM A GREAT TRADER/ I LEARN LESSONS FROM EVERY TRADE AND IMPLEMENT THEM/ I AM A CONSTANTLY IMPROVING TRADER/ I AIM FOR EXCELLENCE IN EVERY TRADE.

DATE _____   TIME _____

DEMO/REAL   INSTRUMENT _____

SETUP
_____
_____
_____

A/B/C GRADE TRADE   RANDOM TRADE?
STOP ADHERED TO Y/N
IF NOT WHY NOT?
_____
_____
_____

TAKE PROFIT ADHERED TO Y/N
IF NOT WHY NOT?
_____
_____
_____

BREAK EVEN ADHERED TO Y/N
IF NOT WHY NOT?
_____
_____
_____

LESSONS I LEARNED FROM THIS TRADE

_____
_____
_____
_____
_____
_____

WIN/LOSS _____
PROFIT % ON ACCOUNT _____
LOSS % ON ACCOUNT _____

HOW WILL I IMPROVE ON MY NEXT TRADE

_____
_____
_____

VISUAL EXCERCISE (5-10 MINUTES)

PUT ON SOME SOFT MUSIC, LAY BACK AND RELAX AND RECREATE THE TRADE IN YOUR MIND'S EYE.

NOW SEE YOURSELF GOING THROUGH A TRADE BUT NOW YOU ARE IMPLEMENTING THE NEW LESSONS LEARNED FROM THIS TRADE. REPEAT UNTIL YOU AUTOMATICALLY ACT THIS WAY DURING TRADES

TRADER AFFIRMATIONS (SAY 100 TIMES A DAY)

I AM A GREAT TRADER/ I LEARN LESSONS FROM EVERY TRADE AND IMPLEMENT THEM/ I AM A CONSTANTLY IMPROVING TRADER/ I AIM FOR EXCELLENCE IN EVERY TRADE.

DATE _____ TIME _____

DEMO/REAL   INSTRUMENT _____

SETUP
_____
_____
_____

A/B/C GRADE TRADE   RANDOM TRADE?

STOP ADHERED TO Y/N

IF NOT WHY NOT?
_____
_____
_____

TAKE PROFIT ADHERED TO Y/N

IF NOT WHY NOT?
_____
_____
_____

BREAK EVEN ADHERED TO Y/N

IF NOT WHY NOT?
_____
_____
_____

LESSONS I LEARNED FROM THIS TRADE

_____
_____
_____
_____
_____
_____

WIN/LOSS _____
PROFIT % ON ACCOUNT _____
LOSS % ON ACCOUNT _____

HOW WILL I IMPROVE ON MY NEXT TRADE
_____
_____
_____

VISUAL EXCERCISE (5-10 MINUTES)

PUT ON SOME SOFT MUSIC, LAY BACK AND RELAX AND RECREATE THE TRADE IN YOUR MIND'S EYE.
NOW SEE YOURSELF GOING THROUGH A TRADE BUT NOW YOU ARE IMPLEMENTING THE NEW LESSONS LEARNED FROM THIS TRADE. REPEAT UNTIL YOU AUTOMATICALLY ACT THIS WAY DURING TRADES

TRADER AFFIRMATIONS (SAY 100 TIMES A DAY)

I AM A GREAT TRADER/ I LEARN LESSONS FROM EVERY TRADE AND IMPLEMENT THEM/ I AM A CONSTANTLY IMPROVING TRADER/ I AIM FOR EXCELLENCE IN EVERY TRADE.

DATE _____   TIME _____

DEMO/REAL   INSTRUMENT _____

SETUP
_____
_____

A/B/C GRADE TRADE   RANDOM TRADE?
STOP ADHERED TO Y/N
IF NOT WHY NOT?
_____
_____

TAKE PROFIT ADHERED TO Y/N
IF NOT WHY NOT?
_____
_____
_____

BREAK EVEN ADHERED TO Y/N
IF NOT WHY NOT?
_____
_____
_____

LESSONS I LEARNED FROM THIS TRADE

_____
_____
_____
_____
_____
_____

WIN/LOSS _____

PROFIT % ON ACCOUNT _____

LOSS % ON ACCOUNT _____

HOW WILL I IMPROVE ON MY NEXT TRADE

_____
_____
_____

VISUAL EXCERCISE (5-10 MINUTES)

PUT ON SOME SOFT MUSIC, LAY BACK AND RELAX AND RECREATE THE TRADE IN YOUR MIND'S EYE.

NOW SEE YOURSELF GOING THROUGH A TRADE BUT NOW YOU ARE IMPLEMENTING THE NEW LESSONS LEARNED FROM THIS TRADE. REPEAT UNTIL YOU AUTOMATICALLY ACT THIS WAY DURING TRADES

TRADER AFFIRMATIONS (SAY 100 TIMES A DAY)

I AM A GREAT TRADER/ I LEARN LESSONS FROM EVERY TRADE AND IMPLEMENT THEM/ I AM A CONSTANTLY IMPROVING TRADER/ I AIM FOR EXCELLENCE IN EVERY TRADE.

DATE _____ TIME _____

DEMO/REAL   INSTRUMENT _____

SETUP
_____
_____
_____

A/B/C GRADE TRADE   RANDOM TRADE?
STOP ADHERED TO Y/N
IF NOT WHY NOT?
_____
_____
_____

TAKE PROFIT ADHERED TO Y/N
IF NOT WHY NOT?
_____
_____
_____

BREAK EVEN ADHERED TO Y/N
IF NOT WHY NOT?
_____
_____
_____

LESSONS I LEARNED FROM THIS TRADE

_____
_____
_____
_____
_____
_____

WIN/LOSS _____

PROFIT % ON ACCOUNT _____

LOSS % ON ACCOUNT _____

HOW WILL I IMPROVE ON MY NEXT TRADE

_____
_____

VISUAL EXCERCISE (5-10 MINUTES)

PUT ON SOME SOFT MUSIC, LAY BACK AND RELAX AND RECREATE THE TRADE IN YOUR MIND'S EYE.

NOW SEE YOURSELF GOING THROUGH A TRADE BUT NOW YOU ARE IMPLEMENTING THE NEW LESSONS LEARNED FROM THIS TRADE. REPEAT UNTIL YOU AUTOMATICALLY ACT THIS WAY DURING TRADES

TRADER AFFIRMATIONS (SAY 100 TIMES A DAY)

I AM A GREAT TRADER/ I LEARN LESSONS FROM EVERY TRADE AND IMPLEMENT THEM/ I AM A CONSTANTLY IMPROVING TRADER/ I AIM FOR EXCELLENCE IN EVERY TRADE.

DATE _____ TIME _____

DEMO/REAL   INSTRUMENT _____

SETUP
_____
_____
_____

A/B/C GRADE TRADE   RANDOM TRADE?

STOP ADHERED TO Y/N

IF NOT WHY NOT?
_____
_____
_____

TAKE PROFIT ADHERED TO Y/N

IF NOT WHY NOT?
_____
_____
_____

BREAK EVEN ADHERED TO Y/N

IF NOT WHY NOT?
_____
_____
_____

LESSONS I LEARNED FROM THIS TRADE

_____
_____
_____
_____
_____

WIN/LOSS _____
PROFIT % ON ACCOUNT _____
LOSS % ON ACCOUNT _____

HOW WILL I IMPROVE ON MY NEXT TRADE

_____
_____
_____

VISUAL EXCERCISE (5-10 MINUTES)

PUT ON SOME SOFT MUSIC, LAY BACK AND RELAX AND RECREATE THE TRADE IN YOUR MIND'S EYE.
NOW SEE YOURSELF GOING THROUGH A TRADE BUT NOW YOU ARE IMPLEMENTING THE NEW LESSONS LEARNED FROM THIS TRADE. REPEAT UNTIL YOU AUTOMATICALLY ACT THIS WAY DURING TRADES

TRADER AFFIRMATIONS (SAY 100 TIMES A DAY)

I AM A GREAT TRADER/ I LEARN LESSONS FROM EVERY TRADE AND IMPLEMENT THEM/ I AM A CONSTANTLY IMPROVING TRADER/ I AIM FOR EXCELLENCE IN EVERY TRADE.

DATE _____ TIME _____

DEMO/REAL INSTRUMENT _____

SETUP
_____
_____
_____

A/B/C GRADE TRADE   RANDOM TRADE?

STOP ADHERED TO Y/N

IF NOT WHY NOT?
_____
_____
_____

TAKE PROFIT ADHERED TO Y/N

IF NOT WHY NOT?
_____
_____
_____

BREAK EVEN ADHERED TO Y/N

IF NOT WHY NOT?
_____
_____
_____

LESSONS I LEARNED FROM THIS TRADE

_____

_____

_____

_____

_____

WIN/LOSS _____

PROFIT % ON ACCOUNT _____

LOSS % ON ACCOUNT _____

HOW WILL I IMPROVE ON MY NEXT TRADE

_____

_____

_____

VISUAL EXCERCISE (5-10 MINUTES)

PUT ON SOME SOFT MUSIC, LAY BACK AND RELAX AND RECREATE THE TRADE IN YOUR MIND'S EYE.

NOW SEE YOURSELF GOING THROUGH A TRADE BUT NOW YOU ARE IMPLEMENTING THE NEW LESSONS LEARNED FROM THIS TRADE. REPEAT UNTIL YOU AUTOMATICALLY ACT THIS WAY DURING TRADES

TRADER AFFIRMATIONS (SAY 100 TIMES A DAY)

I AM A GREAT TRADER/ I LEARN LESSONS FROM EVERY TRADE AND IMPLEMENT THEM/ I AM A CONSTANTLY IMPROVING TRADER/ I AIM FOR EXCELLENCE IN EVERY TRADE.

DATE _____ TIME _____

DEMO/REAL   INSTRUMENT _____

SETUP
_____
_____

_____

A/B/C GRADE TRADE   RANDOM TRADE?
  STOP ADHERED TO Y/N
  IF NOT WHY NOT?

_____
_____

_____

TAKE PROFIT ADHERED TO Y/N
IF NOT WHY NOT?

_____
_____

_____

BREAK EVEN ADHERED TO Y/N
IF NOT WHY NOT?

_____
_____

_____

LESSONS I LEARNED FROM THIS TRADE

_____
_____
_____
_____
_____
_____

WIN/LOSS _____

PROFIT % ON ACCOUNT _____

LOSS % ON ACCOUNT _____

HOW WILL I IMPROVE ON MY NEXT TRADE

_____
_____
_____

VISUAL EXCERCISE (5-10 MINUTES)

PUT ON SOME SOFT MUSIC, LAY BACK AND RELAX AND RECREATE THE TRADE IN YOUR MIND'S EYE.

NOW SEE YOURSELF GOING THROUGH A TRADE BUT NOW YOU ARE IMPLEMENTING THE NEW LESSONS LEARNED FROM THIS TRADE. REPEAT UNTIL YOU AUTOMATICALLY ACT THIS WAY DURING TRADES

TRADER AFFIRMATIONS (SAY 100 TIMES A DAY)

I AM A GREAT TRADER/ I LEARN LESSONS FROM EVERY TRADE AND IMPLEMENT THEM/ I AM A CONSTANTLY IMPROVING TRADER/ I AIM FOR EXCELLENCE IN EVERY TRADE.

DATE _____   TIME _____

DEMO/REAL   INSTRUMENT _____

SETUP
_____
_____

A/B/C GRADE TRADE   RANDOM TRADE?

STOP ADHERED TO Y/N

IF NOT WHY NOT?
_____
_____

TAKE PROFIT ADHERED TO Y/N

IF NOT WHY NOT?
_____
_____
_____

BREAK EVEN ADHERED TO Y/N

IF NOT WHY NOT?
_____
_____
_____

LESSONS I LEARNED FROM THIS TRADE

_____
_____
_____
_____
_____
_____

WIN/LOSS _____

PROFIT % ON ACCOUNT _____

LOSS % ON ACCOUNT _____

HOW WILL I IMPROVE ON MY NEXT TRADE

_____
_____
_____

VISUAL EXCERCISE (5-10 MINUTES)

PUT ON SOME SOFT MUSIC, LAY BACK AND RELAX AND RECREATE THE TRADE IN YOUR MIND'S EYE.

NOW SEE YOURSELF GOING THROUGH A TRADE BUT NOW YOU ARE IMPLEMENTING THE NEW LESSONS LEARNED FROM THIS TRADE. REPEAT UNTIL YOU AUTOMATICALLY ACT THIS WAY DURING TRADES

TRADER AFFIRMATIONS (SAY 100 TIMES A DAY)

I AM A GREAT TRADER/ I LEARN LESSONS FROM EVERY TRADE AND IMPLEMENT THEM/ I AM A CONSTANTLY IMPROVING TRADER/ I AIM FOR EXCELLENCE IN EVERY TRADE.

DATE _____ TIME _____

DEMO/REAL   INSTRUMENT _____

SETUP
_____
_____
_____

A/B/C GRADE TRADE   RANDOM TRADE?
STOP ADHERED TO Y/N
IF NOT WHY NOT?
_____
_____
_____

TAKE PROFIT ADHERED TO Y/N
IF NOT WHY NOT?
_____
_____
_____

BREAK EVEN ADHERED TO Y/N
IF NOT WHY NOT?
_____
_____
_____

LESSONS I LEARNED FROM THIS TRADE

_____
_____
_____
_____
_____

WIN/LOSS _____

PROFIT % ON ACCOUNT _____

LOSS % ON ACCOUNT _____

HOW WILL I IMPROVE ON MY NEXT TRADE

_____
_____
_____

VISUAL EXCERCISE (5-10 MINUTES)

PUT ON SOME SOFT MUSIC, LAY BACK AND RELAX AND RECREATE THE TRADE IN YOUR MIND'S EYE.

NOW SEE YOURSELF GOING THROUGH A TRADE BUT NOW YOU ARE IMPLEMENTING THE NEW LESSONS LEARNED FROM THIS TRADE. REPEAT UNTIL YOU AUTOMATICALLY ACT THIS WAY DURING TRADES

TRADER AFFIRMATIONS (SAY 100 TIMES A DAY)

I AM A GREAT TRADER/ I LEARN LESSONS FROM EVERY TRADE AND IMPLEMENT THEM/ I AM A CONSTANTLY IMPROVING TRADER/ I AIM FOR EXCELLENCE IN EVERY TRADE.

DATE _____ TIME _____

DEMO/REAL   INSTRUMENT _____

SETUP
_____
_____
_____

A/B/C GRADE TRADE   RANDOM TRADE?
STOP ADHERED TO Y/N
IF NOT WHY NOT?
_____
_____
_____

TAKE PROFIT ADHERED TO Y/N
IF NOT WHY NOT?
_____
_____
_____

BREAK EVEN ADHERED TO Y/N
IF NOT WHY NOT?
_____
_____
_____

LESSONS I LEARNED FROM THIS TRADE
_____
_____
_____
_____
_____
_____
_____

WIN/LOSS _____
PROFIT % ON ACCOUNT _____
LOSS % ON ACCOUNT _____

HOW WILL I IMPROVE ON MY NEXT TRADE
_____
_____
_____

VISUAL EXCERCISE (5-10 MINUTES)

PUT ON SOME SOFT MUSIC, LAY BACK AND RELAX AND RECREATE THE TRADE IN YOUR MIND'S EYE.
NOW SEE YOURSELF GOING THROUGH A TRADE BUT NOW YOU ARE IMPLEMENTING THE NEW LESSONS LEARNED FROM THIS TRADE. REPEAT UNTIL YOU AUTOMATICALLY ACT THIS WAY DURING TRADES

TRADER AFFIRMATIONS (SAY 100 TIMES A DAY)

I AM A GREAT TRADER/ I LEARN LESSONS FROM EVERY TRADE AND IMPLEMENT THEM/ I AM A CONSTANTLY IMPROVING TRADER/ I AIM FOR EXCELLENCE IN EVERY TRADE.

DATE _____   TIME _____

DEMO/REAL   INSTRUMENT _____

SETUP
_____
_____
_____

A/B/C GRADE TRADE   RANDOM TRADE?
STOP ADHERED TO Y/N
IF NOT WHY NOT?
_____
_____
_____

TAKE PROFIT ADHERED TO Y/N
IF NOT WHY NOT?
_____
_____
_____

BREAK EVEN ADHERED TO Y/N
IF NOT WHY NOT?
_____
_____
_____

LESSONS I LEARNED FROM THIS TRADE

_____
_____
_____
_____
_____
_____

WIN/LOSS _____

PROFIT % ON ACCOUNT _____

LOSS % ON ACCOUNT _____

HOW WILL I IMPROVE ON MY NEXT TRADE

_____
_____
_____

VISUAL EXCERCISE (5-10 MINUTES)

PUT ON SOME SOFT MUSIC, LAY BACK AND RELAX AND RECREATE THE TRADE IN YOUR MIND'S EYE.

NOW SEE YOURSELF GOING THROUGH A TRADE BUT NOW YOU ARE IMPLEMENTING THE NEW LESSONS LEARNED FROM THIS TRADE. REPEAT UNTIL YOU AUTOMATICALLY ACT THIS WAY DURING TRADES

TRADER AFFIRMATIONS (SAY 100 TIMES A DAY)

I AM A GREAT TRADER/ I LEARN LESSONS FROM EVERY TRADE AND IMPLEMENT THEM/ I AM A CONSTANTLY IMPROVING TRADER/ I AIM FOR EXCELLENCE IN EVERY TRADE.

DATE _____ TIME _____

DEMO/REAL   INSTRUMENT _____

SETUP
_____
_____
_____

A/B/C GRADE TRADE   RANDOM TRADE?
STOP ADHERED TO Y/N
IF NOT WHY NOT?
_____
_____
_____

TAKE PROFIT ADHERED TO Y/N
IF NOT WHY NOT?
_____
_____
_____

BREAK EVEN ADHERED TO Y/N
IF NOT WHY NOT?
_____
_____
_____

LESSONS I LEARNED FROM THIS TRADE

_____
_____
_____
_____
_____
_____

WIN/LOSS _____
PROFIT % ON ACCOUNT _____
LOSS % ON ACCOUNT _____

HOW WILL I IMPROVE ON MY NEXT TRADE
_____
_____
_____

VISUAL EXCERCISE (5-10 MINUTES)

PUT ON SOME SOFT MUSIC, LAY BACK AND RELAX AND RECREATE THE TRADE IN YOUR MIND'S EYE.
NOW SEE YOURSELF GOING THROUGH A TRADE BUT NOW YOU ARE IMPLEMENTING THE NEW LESSONS LEARNED FROM THIS TRADE. REPEAT UNTIL YOU AUTOMATICALLY ACT THIS WAY DURING TRADES

TRADER AFFIRMATIONS (SAY 100 TIMES A DAY)

I AM A GREAT TRADER/ I LEARN LESSONS FROM EVERY TRADE AND IMPLEMENT THEM/ I AM A CONSTANTLY IMPROVING TRADER/ I AIM FOR EXCELLENCE IN EVERY TRADE.

DATE _____ TIME _____

DEMO/REAL   INSTRUMENT _____

SETUP
_____
_____
_____

A/B/C GRADE TRADE   RANDOM TRADE?

STOP ADHERED TO Y/N

IF NOT WHY NOT?
_____
_____
_____

TAKE PROFIT ADHERED TO Y/N

IF NOT WHY NOT?
_____
_____
_____

BREAK EVEN ADHERED TO Y/N

IF NOT WHY NOT?
_____
_____
_____

LESSONS I LEARNED FROM THIS TRADE

_____

_____

_____

_____

_____

_____

WIN/LOSS _____

PROFIT % ON ACCOUNT _____

LOSS % ON ACCOUNT _____

HOW WILL I IMPROVE ON MY NEXT TRADE

_____

_____

_____

VISUAL EXCERCISE (5-10 MINUTES)

PUT ON SOME SOFT MUSIC, LAY BACK AND RELAX AND RECREATE THE TRADE IN YOUR MIND'S EYE.

NOW SEE YOURSELF GOING THROUGH A TRADE BUT NOW YOU ARE IMPLEMENTING THE NEW LESSONS LEARNED FROM THIS TRADE. REPEAT UNTIL YOU AUTOMATICALLY ACT THIS WAY DURING TRADES

TRADER AFFIRMATIONS (SAY 100 TIMES A DAY)

I AM A GREAT TRADER/ I LEARN LESSONS FROM EVERY TRADE AND IMPLEMENT THEM/ I AM A CONSTANTLY IMPROVING TRADER/ I AIM FOR EXCELLENCE IN EVERY TRADE.

DATE _____   TIME _____

DEMO/REAL   INSTRUMENT _____

SETUP
_____
_____
_____

A/B/C GRADE TRADE   RANDOM TRADE?

STOP ADHERED TO Y/N

IF NOT WHY NOT?
_____
_____
_____

TAKE PROFIT ADHERED TO Y/N

IF NOT WHY NOT?
_____
_____
_____

BREAK EVEN ADHERED TO Y/N

IF NOT WHY NOT?
_____
_____
_____

LESSONS I LEARNED FROM THIS TRADE

_____
_____
_____
_____
_____

WIN/LOSS _____

PROFIT % ON ACCOUNT _____

LOSS % ON ACCOUNT _____

HOW WILL I IMPROVE ON MY NEXT TRADE

_____
_____
_____

VISUAL EXCERCISE (5-10 MINUTES)

PUT ON SOME SOFT MUSIC, LAY BACK AND RELAX AND RECREATE THE TRADE IN YOUR MIND'S EYE.

NOW SEE YOURSELF GOING THROUGH A TRADE BUT NOW YOU ARE IMPLEMENTING THE NEW LESSONS LEARNED FROM THIS TRADE. REPEAT UNTIL YOU AUTOMATICALLY ACT THIS WAY DURING TRADES

TRADER AFFIRMATIONS (SAY 100 TIMES A DAY)

I AM A GREAT TRADER/ I LEARN LESSONS FROM EVERY TRADE AND IMPLEMENT THEM/ I AM A CONSTANTLY IMPROVING TRADER/ I AIM FOR EXCELLENCE IN EVERY TRADE.

DATE _____   TIME _____

DEMO/REAL   INSTRUMENT _____

SETUP
_____
_____
_____

A/B/C GRADE TRADE   RANDOM TRADE?

STOP ADHERED TO Y/N

IF NOT WHY NOT?
_____
_____
_____

TAKE PROFIT ADHERED TO Y/N

IF NOT WHY NOT?
_____
_____
_____

BREAK EVEN ADHERED TO Y/N

IF NOT WHY NOT?
_____
_____
_____

LESSONS I LEARNED FROM THIS TRADE

_____
_____
_____
_____
_____

WIN/LOSS _____

PROFIT % ON ACCOUNT _____

LOSS % ON ACCOUNT _____

HOW WILL I IMPROVE ON MY NEXT TRADE

_____
_____
_____

VISUAL EXCERCISE (5-10 MINUTES)

PUT ON SOME SOFT MUSIC, LAY BACK AND RELAX AND RECREATE THE TRADE IN YOUR MIND'S EYE.

NOW SEE YOURSELF GOING THROUGH A TRADE BUT NOW YOU ARE IMPLEMENTING THE NEW LESSONS LEARNED FROM THIS TRADE. REPEAT UNTIL YOU AUTOMATICALLY ACT THIS WAY DURING TRADES

TRADER AFFIRMATIONS (SAY 100 TIMES A DAY)

I AM A GREAT TRADER/ I LEARN LESSONS FROM EVERY TRADE AND IMPLEMENT THEM/ I AM A CONSTANTLY IMPROVING TRADER/ I AIM FOR EXCELLENCE IN EVERY TRADE.

DATE _____ TIME _____

DEMO/REAL   INSTRUMENT _____

SETUP
_____
_____
_____

A/B/C GRADE TRADE   RANDOM TRADE?

STOP ADHERED TO Y/N

IF NOT WHY NOT?
_____
_____
_____

TAKE PROFIT ADHERED TO Y/N

IF NOT WHY NOT?
_____
_____
_____

BREAK EVEN ADHERED TO Y/N

IF NOT WHY NOT?
_____
_____
_____

LESSONS I LEARNED FROM THIS TRADE

_____
_____
_____
_____
_____

WIN/LOSS _____

PROFIT % ON ACCOUNT _____

LOSS % ON ACCOUNT _____

HOW WILL I IMPROVE ON MY NEXT TRADE

_____
_____
_____

VISUAL EXCERCISE (5-10 MINUTES)

PUT ON SOME SOFT MUSIC, LAY BACK AND RELAX AND RECREATE THE TRADE IN YOUR MIND'S EYE.

NOW SEE YOURSELF GOING THROUGH A TRADE BUT NOW YOU ARE IMPLEMENTING THE NEW LESSONS LEARNED FROM THIS TRADE. REPEAT UNTIL YOU AUTOMATICALLY ACT THIS WAY DURING TRADES

TRADER AFFIRMATIONS (SAY 100 TIMES A DAY)

I AM A GREAT TRADER/ I LEARN LESSONS FROM EVERY TRADE AND IMPLEMENT THEM/ I AM A CONSTANTLY IMPROVING TRADER/ I AIM FOR EXCELLENCE IN EVERY TRADE.

DATE _____ TIME _____

DEMO/REAL   INSTRUMENT _____

SETUP
_____
_____

_____

A/B/C GRADE TRADE   RANDOM TRADE?

STOP ADHERED TO Y/N

IF NOT WHY NOT?
_____
_____

_____

TAKE PROFIT ADHERED TO Y/N

IF NOT WHY NOT?
_____
_____

_____

BREAK EVEN ADHERED TO Y/N

IF NOT WHY NOT?
_____
_____

_____

LESSONS I LEARNED FROM THIS TRADE

_____
_____
_____
_____
_____
_____

WIN/LOSS _____
PROFIT % ON ACCOUNT _____
LOSS % ON ACCOUNT _____

HOW WILL I IMPROVE ON MY NEXT TRADE
_____
_____
_____

VISUAL EXCERCISE (5-10 MINUTES)

PUT ON SOME SOFT MUSIC, LAY BACK AND RELAX AND RECREATE THE TRADE IN YOUR MIND'S EYE.

NOW SEE YOURSELF GOING THROUGH A TRADE BUT NOW YOU ARE IMPLEMENTING THE NEW LESSONS LEARNED FROM THIS TRADE. REPEAT UNTIL YOU AUTOMATICALLY ACT THIS WAY DURING TRADES

TRADER AFFIRMATIONS (SAY 100 TIMES A DAY)

I AM A GREAT TRADER/ I LEARN LESSONS FROM EVERY TRADE AND IMPLEMENT THEM/ I AM A CONSTANTLY IMPROVING TRADER/ I AIM FOR EXCELLENCE IN EVERY TRADE.

DATE _____ TIME _____

DEMO/REAL   INSTRUMENT _____

SETUP
_____
_____
_____

A/B/C GRADE TRADE   RANDOM TRADE?
  STOP ADHERED TO Y/N
  IF NOT WHY NOT?
_____
_____
_____

TAKE PROFIT ADHERED TO Y/N
IF NOT WHY NOT?
_____
_____
_____

BREAK EVEN ADHERED TO Y/N
IF NOT WHY NOT?
_____
_____
_____

LESSONS I LEARNED FROM THIS TRADE

_____
_____
_____
_____
_____
_____

WIN/LOSS _____
PROFIT % ON ACCOUNT _____
LOSS % ON ACCOUNT _____

HOW WILL I IMPROVE ON MY NEXT TRADE
_____
_____
_____

VISUAL EXCERCISE (5-10 MINUTES)

PUT ON SOME SOFT MUSIC, LAY BACK AND RELAX AND RECREATE THE TRADE IN YOUR MIND'S EYE.

NOW SEE YOURSELF GOING THROUGH A TRADE BUT NOW YOU ARE IMPLEMENTING THE NEW LESSONS LEARNED FROM THIS TRADE. REPEAT UNTIL YOU AUTOMATICALLY ACT THIS WAY DURING TRADES

TRADER AFFIRMATIONS (SAY 100 TIMES A DAY)

I AM A GREAT TRADER/ I LEARN LESSONS FROM EVERY TRADE AND IMPLEMENT THEM/ I AM A CONSTANTLY IMPROVING TRADER/ I AIM FOR EXCELLENCE IN EVERY TRADE.

DATE _____ TIME _____

DEMO/REAL   INSTRUMENT _____

SETUP
_____
_____
_____

A/B/C GRADE TRADE   RANDOM TRADE?

STOP ADHERED TO Y/N

IF NOT WHY NOT?
_____
_____
_____

TAKE PROFIT ADHERED TO Y/N

IF NOT WHY NOT?
_____
_____
_____

BREAK EVEN ADHERED TO Y/N

IF NOT WHY NOT?
_____
_____
_____

LESSONS I LEARNED FROM THIS TRADE

_____
_____
_____
_____
_____
_____

WIN/LOSS _____

PROFIT % ON ACCOUNT _____

LOSS % ON ACCOUNT _____

HOW WILL I IMPROVE ON MY NEXT TRADE

_____
_____
_____

VISUAL EXCERCISE (5-10 MINUTES)

PUT ON SOME SOFT MUSIC, LAY BACK AND RELAX AND RECREATE THE TRADE IN YOUR MIND'S EYE.

NOW SEE YOURSELF GOING THROUGH A TRADE BUT NOW YOU ARE IMPLEMENTING THE NEW LESSONS LEARNED FROM THIS TRADE. REPEAT UNTIL YOU AUTOMATICALLY ACT THIS WAY DURING TRADES

TRADER AFFIRMATIONS (SAY 100 TIMES A DAY)

I AM A GREAT TRADER/ I LEARN LESSONS FROM EVERY TRADE AND IMPLEMENT THEM/ I AM A CONSTANTLY IMPROVING TRADER/ I AIM FOR EXCELLENCE IN EVERY TRADE.

DATE _____ TIME _____

DEMO/REAL   INSTRUMENT _____

SETUP
_____
_____
_____

A/B/C GRADE TRADE   RANDOM TRADE?

STOP ADHERED TO Y/N

IF NOT WHY NOT?
_____
_____
_____

TAKE PROFIT ADHERED TO Y/N

IF NOT WHY NOT?
_____
_____
_____

BREAK EVEN ADHERED TO Y/N

IF NOT WHY NOT?
_____
_____
_____

LESSONS I LEARNED FROM THIS TRADE

_____
_____
_____
_____
_____
_____

WIN/LOSS _____

PROFIT % ON ACCOUNT _____

LOSS % ON ACCOUNT _____

HOW WILL I IMPROVE ON MY NEXT TRADE

_____
_____
_____

VISUAL EXCERCISE (5-10 MINUTES)

PUT ON SOME SOFT MUSIC, LAY BACK AND RELAX AND RECREATE THE TRADE IN YOUR MIND'S EYE.

NOW SEE YOURSELF GOING THROUGH A TRADE BUT NOW YOU ARE IMPLEMENTING THE NEW LESSONS LEARNED FROM THIS TRADE. REPEAT UNTIL YOU AUTOMATICALLY ACT THIS WAY DURING TRADES

TRADER AFFIRMATIONS (SAY 100 TIMES A DAY)

I AM A GREAT TRADER/ I LEARN LESSONS FROM EVERY TRADE AND IMPLEMENT THEM/ I AM A CONSTANTLY IMPROVING TRADER/ I AIM FOR EXCELLENCE IN EVERY TRADE.

DATE _____ TIME _____

DEMO/REAL   INSTRUMENT _____

SETUP
_____
_____
_____

A/B/C GRADE TRADE   RANDOM TRADE?
  STOP ADHERED TO Y/N
  IF NOT WHY NOT?
_____
_____
_____

TAKE PROFIT ADHERED TO Y/N
IF NOT WHY NOT?
_____
_____
_____

BREAK EVEN ADHERED TO Y/N
IF NOT WHY NOT?
_____
_____
_____

LESSONS I LEARNED FROM THIS TRADE

_____
_____
_____
_____
_____

WIN/LOSS _____
PROFIT % ON ACCOUNT _____
LOSS % ON ACCOUNT _____

HOW WILL I IMPROVE ON MY NEXT TRADE

_____
_____
_____

VISUAL EXCERCISE (5-10 MINUTES)

PUT ON SOME SOFT MUSIC, LAY BACK AND RELAX AND RECREATE THE TRADE IN YOUR MIND'S EYE.

NOW SEE YOURSELF GOING THROUGH A TRADE BUT NOW YOU ARE IMPLEMENTING THE NEW LESSONS LEARNED FROM THIS TRADE. REPEAT UNTIL YOU AUTOMATICALLY ACT THIS WAY DURING TRADES

TRADER AFFIRMATIONS (SAY 100 TIMES A DAY)

I AM A GREAT TRADER/ I LEARN LESSONS FROM EVERY TRADE AND IMPLEMENT THEM/ I AM A CONSTANTLY IMPROVING TRADER/ I AIM FOR EXCELLENCE IN EVERY TRADE.

DATE _____ TIME _____

DEMO/REAL   INSTRUMENT _____

SETUP
_____
_____
_____

A/B/C GRADE TRADE   RANDOM TRADE?
STOP ADHERED TO Y/N
IF NOT WHY NOT?
_____
_____
_____

TAKE PROFIT ADHERED TO Y/N
IF NOT WHY NOT?
_____
_____
_____

BREAK EVEN ADHERED TO Y/N
IF NOT WHY NOT?
_____
_____
_____

LESSONS I LEARNED FROM THIS TRADE

_____

_____

_____

_____

_____

WIN/LOSS _____

PROFIT % ON ACCOUNT _____

LOSS % ON ACCOUNT _____

HOW WILL I IMPROVE ON MY NEXT TRADE

_____

_____

VISUAL EXCERCISE (5-10 MINUTES)

PUT ON SOME SOFT MUSIC, LAY BACK AND RELAX AND RECREATE THE TRADE IN YOUR MIND'S EYE.

NOW SEE YOURSELF GOING THROUGH A TRADE BUT NOW YOU ARE IMPLEMENTING THE NEW LESSONS LEARNED FROM THIS TRADE. REPEAT UNTIL YOU AUTOMATICALLY ACT THIS WAY DURING TRADES

TRADER AFFIRMATIONS (SAY 100 TIMES A DAY)

I AM A GREAT TRADER/ I LEARN LESSONS FROM EVERY TRADE AND IMPLEMENT THEM/ I AM A CONSTANTLY IMPROVING TRADER/ I AIM FOR EXCELLENCE IN EVERY TRADE.

CONGRATULATIONS

YOU HAVE RECORDED 100 TRADES!

KEEP UP THE GOOD WORK BY ORDERING YOUR NEXT JOURNAL (WHY DON'T YOU ORDER 2 OR 3, SO YOU NEVER RUN OUT!)

ALL THE BEST AND GOOD TRADING

LR THOMAS

HTTP://TRADERSELFCONTROL.COM/KEEP-A-TRADING-JOURNAL/

REVIEWS

IF YOU FIND THIS JOURNAL USEFUL PLEASE LEAVE A REVIEW ON AMAZON FOR OTHERS TO READ.

AS A THANK YOU, YOU CAN GET A PDF COPY OF ANY OF MY TRADING BOOKS, JUST EMAIL

lrthomasauthor@gmail.com

JUST SEND ME THE LINK TO THE REVIEW, AND STATE THE BOOK YOU WANT.

BOOKS BY LR THOMAS

TRADING PSYCHOLOGY

- CONTROL YOUR INNER TRADER
- OVERCOME YOUR FEAR IN TRADING
- HOW TO STOP OVER-TRADING
- PATIENCE
- THE TRADING PSYCHOLOGY COLLECTION

HTTP://TRADERSELFCONTROL.COM/EBOOKS/

'CREATE YOUR TRADING SUCCESS'

VIDEO COURSE

HTTP://TRADERSELFCONTROL.COM/

'CREATE YOUR TRADING SUCCESS' COACHING/THERAPY

IF YOU FEEL YOU NEED SOME MORE SPECIALIZED ONE-ON-ONE HELP, YOU CAN FIND OUT MORE ABOUT MY SERVICES AT...

http://traderselfcontrol.com/coaching-services

BOOKS BY LR THOMAS

HIGH ROI TRADING

- THE 10XROI TRADING SYSTEM
- THE TRADE AROUND YOUR JOB SYSTEM
- THE HIGH ROI SCALPING SYSTEM
- THE HIGH ROI END OF DAY SYSTEM

HTTP://10XROITRADINGSYSTEM.COM/THE-EBOOKS/

COURSES BY LR THOMAS

HIGH ROI DAY TRADING
http://day.10xroitradingsystem.com/

HIGH ROI SWING TRADING
http://highroicourse.10xroitradingsystem.com/

HIGH ROI END OF DAY TRADING
http://highroicourse.10xroitradingsystem.com/

CATCH THE HUGE MARKET MOVES
http://10xroitradingsystem.com/huge-market-moves/

MARKET RHYTHMS
http://10xroitradingsystem.com/learn-how-to-profit-with-market-rhythms/

CREATE YOUR TRADING SUCCESS
http://traderselfcontrol.com/

TRADING JOURNAL NOTES

TRADING JOURNAL NOTES

Made in the USA
Middletown, DE
11 January 2021